Techno Rebels

Techno Rebels

The Renegades of
Electronic Funk

SECOND EDITION
REVISED AND UPDATED

Dan Sicko

WITH A FOREWORD BY BILL BREWSTER

A PAINTED TURTLE BOOK
DETROIT, MICHIGAN

© 2010 by Wayne State University Press, Detroit, Michigan 48201.
All rights reserved. No part of this book may be reproduced without formal permission.
Manufactured in the United States of America.

Library of Congress Cataloging-in-Publication Data

Sicko, Dan.
Techno rebels : the renegades of electronic funk / Dan Sicko ; with a foreword by
Bill Brewster. — 2nd ed.
p. cm.
Includes bibliographical references and index.
ISBN 978-0-8143-3438-6 (pbk. : alk. paper)
1. Techno music—History and criticism.   I. Title.
ML3540.S53 2010
781.66—dc22

2009033759
∞
Designed by Isaac Tobin
Typeset by The Composing Room of Michigan, Inc.
Composed in Minion Pro and Courier

Contents

Foreword

History is bunk, said that old Detroit pioneer, Henry Ford, and he may well have been talking about techno rather than motor cars. Since techno left Michigan and headed out east it has been widely misunderstood while critics have merrily deracinated its origins to the point where plenty probably still believe it began in Holland when Tiësto's mum gave birth to a cute-as-a-button trance superstar.

Most of Detroit's musical past is well documented, from John Lee Hooker's urban blues to the modern jazz of Elvin Jones and Milt Jackson; the gospel of Aretha and the Clark Sisters, the hard rock of MC5, Bob Seger and Ted Nugent and Tamla Motown's conveyor belt of soul stars. But techno? Well, of course we know it really comes from Detroit and that its pioneers were Derrick May, Juan Atkins, and Kevin Saunderson. Beyond that is a hinterland of conjecture and supposition.

Devoid of any bands, swimming pool–based antics, and, crucially, lyrics, dance music has often been ill served by its writers, who either seem keen to regurgitate cultural theory master's theses as plain truth or get basic facts wrong (the Paradise Garage in New Jersey, anyone?). And rarely has a genre of music been so misinterpreted as techno.

Occasionally, though, a book comes along that not only enlightens and entertains but also makes you change the way you think about its subject. Dan Sicko's *Techno Rebels,* first published in 1999, wrested techno's history from its European pillagers and handed the history back to its rightful owner: Detroit, the Motor City.

Not only that, but he presented a powerful argument that Detroit was no mere minor adjunct to its more vocal Midwest counterpart, Chicago, but asserted Detroit's role as the home *and* incubator of techno. A Detroit insider, Sicko detailed the primary influence of DJs and producers like the Electrifying Mojo, Ken Collier, The Wizard, and Richard Davis and took us into a world of high school parties, electronic bleepery, and questionable Italian fashions that was a world apart from anything happening in New York or Los Angeles. (For a glimpse of this era, go to YouTube and type in "Sharevari" and "The Scene," the local TV dance show.)

Of course, while techno's roots are firmly in Detroit, it had to travel elsewhere to make the impact its innovation surely deserved. It was in the UK and Europe where techno crossed into pop charts, made stars (however temporarily) of Kevin Saunderson, Derrick May, and Juan Atkins, and sowed the seeds for a fresh revolution that coincided with Berlin's walls crumbling into dust.

If Europe is where techno's impact was most greatly felt, it's also arguable that it is also where its soul was lost. Sicko's book follows techno's trail as it hits Britain and Germany before ending back in the United States, where it was briefly sold to the public as part its ill-conceived "electronica" boom (a dark period when Detroit's viscerating rhythms were somehow lumped in with Dirty Vegas's dance-pop and the Prodigy's electro-pantomime). In this new edition of his 1999 classic, Sicko delves deeper into Detroit's role in the development of techno and asks crucial questions such as how The Wizard became Jeff Mills and what the blazes were Magazine 60 singing about on Don Quichotte.

Sicko is never afraid to throw in cultural theory where it's relevant, but *Techno Rebels* is, first, a book grounded in hard facts, common sense, and a real storyteller's eye for the truth. In a market saturated with ill-informed cash-ins and overwrought academic theories, *Techno Rebels* is a classic of its kind.

Bill Brewster, www.djhistory.com

Preface

I HAD BEEN AWAY FROM ICELAND FOR OVER A YEAR AND WHEN I
RETURNED FOR NEW YEAR I STAYED ON TOP OF A MOUNTAIN. I WENT
FOR A WALK ON MY OWN AND I SAW THE ICE WAS THAWING IN THE
LAVA FIELDS. ALL I COULD HEAR WAS THE CACKLE OF THE ICE,
ECHOING OVER HUNDREDS OF SQUARE MILES. IT WAS PITCH BLACK,
THE NORTHERN LIGHTS WERE SWIRLING AROUND AND JUST BELOW
THEM WAS A LAYER OF THICK CLOUD. I COULD SEE THE LIGHTS
FROM ALL THE TOWNS OF MY CHILDHOOD MIRRORED IN THE
REFLECTION OF THESE CLOUDS, WITH THE LAVA FIELDS CACKLING
BELOW. IT WAS REALLY TECHNO.

BJÖRK GUDMUNDSDÓTTIR

It's been ten years, and I've still got a major crush on Björk. Well, at least her unwavering championing of electronic music and her casual use of "techno" as an adjective. Granted, using the word to describe geological events in Iceland is a long way away from assigning it to a type of music or the culture that goes with it.

I'm far less sure of the usefulness of genres these days, but the question "What is techno?" is still one worth answering. *Techno Rebels* will always be an attempt to provide definition, but maybe not in the way you or Wikipedia might expect. I can't apologize for tethering techno to Detroit, a city that in retrospect seems less likely to spawn such a movement with each passing day. The post-industrial entropy is nearly palpable here, while

Hollywood readies sound stages around its perimeter. To put it mildly, it is surreal. Detroit's history, its sense of place and purpose, are all about to be recast. There's never been a bigger need to explore Detroit's innumerable and improbable cultural contributions—if not for the fans and students of music, then for the city itself. While its past is quickly discarded, Detroit needs to remember its future.

Even after the Detroit techno story became more commonly known, I was still amazed by how precious its origins really were. And now, I understand much more its necessity, both for teenagers in the early 1980s and for a city grasping at identity in the twenty first century. Revisiting *Techno Rebels* now means an almost inescapable macro-view of this relationship, a look back at the "collective dreaming" of the city and how it has helped keep the music alive and thriving.

Suffice it to say, it was easy to know what *not* to include in this edition. I specifically chose not to explore techno music's relationship with the "rave" concept and the drug ecstasy, and I stick by my decision. I still believe that it detracts far too greatly from the discussion of the music. Nor will you find any more information, schematics, or wiring diagrams of vintage synthesizers, or screenshots of the latest version of Ableton Live. Each piece of hardware or software feature contributes something to the sonic definition of techno, but not nearly as much as the city borders in which the artists wield them.

Yes, this edition tells more of the "Detroit" story. If it were up to me last time around, I would have stayed in chapter 2 and not come up for air until I had cross-referenced every last Italian disco record and Detroit high school social club. Thankfully for all of us, there's a bit more to discuss. Jeff Mills's transformation into "The Wizard" is something I can finally get into in more detail, and it helps introduce a topic that didn't bubble up as much as I thought it would in the first edition. I'm talking about Ann Arbor, Detroit's nerdier younger brother. Aside from scanning through microfilm of the *Ann Arbor News* for pictures of Cybotron, and that fun little anomaly known as "the Belleville Three," it wasn't worth taking *Techno Rebels* too far west of Detroit. Now it makes a lot more sense once you consider WCBN, Mojo's beginnings, and the emergence of Ghostly International.

A lot more time was spent exploring the mid-1990s this time out, specifically the Detroit party scene that sustained what little infrastructure existed once techno started propagating around the world, and almost single-handedly defined it ever since. If I leaned a little too heavily on techno's pre-history before, the more modern viewpoint of its many promoters should offer some balance.

It would also be an understatement to say that much has happened since 1999: Detroit's Electronic Music Festival, Ghostly, the steady migration of musicians to Berlin, and the birth and death of dozens of subgenres. All but the last inform a retooled chapter 6. What was once a rather terse world tour through some of the techno scenes of the day has given way to the dynamics of how the "idea" of Detroit techno has turned into something very functional and concrete. Maybe now that the "electronica" buzz has played out to be the sideshow it always seemed to be, discussing the music I love will be that much easier.

Thank you to everyone who made this edition possible, especially Amy, Anabel, Rob "Lifecoach" Theakston, Dave Walker, Aran Parillo, Matt MacQueen, Bill Brewster, Ben Mullins, Chris Petersen, Andy Wotta, Jen Hansen, Pete Jacokes and the entire Detroit improv community, Jeff Mills, Sam Valenti IV, Jason Huvaere, Brian Gillespie, Derek Plaslaiko, Peter Wohelski, Marsel Van Der Wielen, Dan Gresham, Jeremy "Sinistarr" Howard, Jon Santos, Brendan Gillen, Doug Coombe, Todd Johnson, Hassan Nurullah, Clark Warner, Liz Warner, Ian Malbon, Hans Veneman, Eddie Otchere, Phil Knott, Gary Arnett, "jm3" (John Manoogian III), Kathy Wildfong, Kristin Harpster Lawrence and all at WSU Press, Matt Becker, Dogfish Head brewery, the Hospital Records podcast, WFMU, and all those hunting down used copies.

1

Welcome to the Machine

America Wakes Up
to Techno, 1997–2010

Don't turn your back on the media—they're liable to hit you upside the head with a new buzzword. Even the casual reader of entertainment news should recognize the term "electronica," the subject of dozens of articles, columns, and news scripts since 1997, all hailing it as the latest music form to usurp rock 'n' roll's stagnant rule.

A convenient media contrivance, "electronica" was concocted to encompass styles as varied as reconfigured disco, minimal and abstracted analog grooves, instrumental hip-hop, melodic synth-pop, the splintered rhythms of "drum 'n' bass"—just about everything that wears the badge of electronic production on its sleeve. While "electronica" works well for categorizing, marketing, and cashing in on the general electronic phenomenon, it precludes any true understanding of the music's details, anecdotes, and minutiae. Each individual style suffers under the electronica umbrella, but none more than techno, the genre that has had the most impact worldwide and has the largest story to tell.

Techno spread to more countries and cultures faster than any music genre in recent history. In Japan, techno artist Ken Ishii was commissioned to write the opening and closing themes for the 1998 Winter Olympics in Nagano. In the Netherlands, Speedy J's "Pull Over" hit the Top 40 in 1990. On July 2, 2005, Detroit techno pioneer Jeff Mills performed several of his works in Pont du Gard, France, accompanied by the seventy-piece Montpellier Philharmonic Orchestra. In November 2008, he was awarded the Legion of Honor by the French government. That same year, Carl Craig and Moritz von Oswald "recomposed" material from recordings of Ravel's *Bolero* and Modest Mussorgsky for Deutsche Grammophon. And in Germany, the massive, twenty-year-old Love Parade—an annual street festival featuring nonstop electronic dance music—continues to attract millions of participants each year.

Even Detroit, the spiritual if not technical home to techno music, has now seen its tenth electronic music festival in Hart Plaza along the Detroit River.

Techno has also become increasingly noticeable in the world of film, picking up steam with the work of Englishman Danny Boyle. The introduction to Boyle's 1994 film *Shallow Grave* and the pivotal emotional finish of his 1996 film *Trainspotting* feature the music of Leftfield and Underworld, respectively. American films have tended to opt for the compilation-friendly "soundtrack," like that of *Blade,* rather than an entire score written by one artist. There have been some interesting exceptions, however, including Orbital's energetic theme for the 1997 film *The Saint* (a reworking of the theme from the old TV show of the same name) and a clever interweaving of techno and narrative in 1998's *Pi.*

Advertising agencies also latched on tightly, putting electronica to work in television commercials. A commercial for the Mitsubishi Eclipse began airing in 2002 with "Days Go By" by the group Dirty Vegas providing the soundtrack for a "pop-locking" front passenger. Whether Dirty Vegas's music was "techno" per se or what spontaneous dancing had to do with selling cars didn't seem to matter. A Model 500 song was used to market the Ford Focus; Hummer was propped up on the music of Matthew Dear;

and Dabrye's beats found their way into a Motorola commercial. America was getting conditioned to electronic sounds, if not developing an affinity for them.

Traditionally, American audiences have had to look and listen a little harder for techno than have their international peers. That all changed in 1997, however, with the electronica explosion and the advent of MTV's weekly late-night show *Amp*. *Amp* tethered the beat of techno to memorable images, giving the music its first mainstream exposure. Along with the all-night outdoor electronica festival known as Organic,[1] *Amp* proved to be one of techno's most compelling outlets in the United States at the time.

Techno was also given play in the United States with Iara Lee's 1998 film *Modulations*, a series of vignettes that loosely traces the development of electronic music from 1910 to the present. Lee's ninety-minute narrative pans the music's continuum, from the industrial noise of Luigi Russolo in 1913 to the turntable kinetics of the Invisbl Skratch Piklz in the late 1990s. By the time the film was made, techno had had at least a decade to mutate and procreate, all of which Lee valiantly attempted to encapsulate.

The specific story of Detroit's contribution has been documented on film with Gary Bredow's *High Tech Soul* in 2006 and mounted as a techno music exhibit titled "Techno: Detroit's Gift to the World" at the Detroit Historical Museum from January 2003 to August 2004. Explorations into techno's past have at the very least begun to embrace some of its unique circumstances, rather than blending everything into a paragraph-sized appetizer.

Media Muddling

But most media entities have danced around the periphery, even with decades of history in which to delve, and the bulk of the music's coverage has been left to the mercies of rock 'n' roll journalism—a world where faith in the dynamic of "bands" determines which artists get added to the carefully pruned tree of rock history. Techno still suffers in this media sphere —though dance music is produced and evolves at a faster rate than most other genres, there's not often much of a *story* to match that pace. Techno has personalities, to be sure, but generally lacks the "rockisms" that make for sensational stories. Drug binges, intra-band squabbles, and hotel anarchy are rarities (and when they do arise, they suddenly seem less glamorous than when initiated by rock stars).

Contributing to techno's sketchy coverage is the media's perpetual quest for the "new." Ironically, it was this quest that helped generate interest in techno and electronica in the first place: by the late 1990s, rock 'n' roll had begun showing wrinkles and age spots; next to this awkward, out-of-touch codger, any seemingly new genre would thrive for a few months. This tendency to pounce whenever the scent of the "next big thing" is in the air is usually a healthy one, allowing new artists and sounds a disproportionate amount of attention for a brief time. But such expediency may also obscure a music's cultural context, which is necessary for a full understanding of its ideas.

Even MTV's *Amp* made little attempt to build an informed audience. The show, which aired from 1997 to 2001, made the strange artistic decision to air without a host or narrator. No interviews were included, and superimposed artist and label information was shown only *after* each song had finished playing. (MTV usually shows this information at both the beginning and end of a song.) All of this, along with some intriguing interstitials,[2] made the show a kind of "video mix," aping the context of a DJ set. What MTV needed to program was something more like its own *Rockumentary*—an attempt to catch its audience up on the wealth of information surrounding the music.

This lack of in-depth coverage isn't unique to techno—coverage of the Pacific Northwest's "grunge" scene between 1989 and 1991 was similarly rushed and cursory. Doug Pray's brilliant and acerbic 1996 documentary *Hype!* put this land of superficiality on trial, showing how both the press and the music industry tried to sum up decades of musical development with only one or two acts and the ephemeral chic of flannel. (As the film explained, people wear flannel clothing in Seattle because it's *cold and rainy*, not because they're trendsetters.) A dismayed Eddie Vedder of Pearl Jam gave the best and simplest critique of grunge's press coverage: "They [the press] made a mistake. . . . They didn't go further and check out other bands."[3]

Brothers and Systems

The U.S. music industry really started noticing techno after New York's Astralwerks, a semi-autonomous branch of Virgin Records, brought the Chemical Brothers' 1995 album *Exit Planet Dust* to American audiences, giving English band members Tom Rowlands and Ed Simons their first break in the United States. Only a few years later, the group's 1997 album

Dig Your Own Hole had gone gold in the United States and platinum world-wide, with one track—"Block Rockin' Beats"—winning the 1998 Grammy Award for best rock instrumental.

While the Chemical Brothers worked hard for their success, part of it can also be attributed to the American music industry's "two years of flat music sales and the sense that 'alternative rock' is flagging"[4]—a general slump in 1995 and 1996, if you will. Artists like Rowlands and Simons came along at the right time, when major labels had begun searching for anti-dotes. Another explanation comes in the logical backlash against pretense, especially among the young—finally, the culture of media saturation had reached its saturation point. Unlike rock 'n' roll, techno is a genre that directs attention solely to its music—live performance challenges, DJ groupies, and trainspotters aside. Audiences don't have lyrics to memo-rize or exaggerated personalities to follow—two of the more standard mar-keting concepts of old. The corollary, of course, is that audiences must do more work than they have in the past. As Peter Wohelski, Astralwerks's former director of A&R, explains, "This is *not* music for the masses."

But whatever the consumer behaviors and underlying social shifts, the success of *Exit Planet Dust* and other records from early English electronic artists did cause a stir in the music industry. Instantly, A&R troops were corralled and ordered to find anything resembling these unassuming acts out of England. Not long after the Chemical Brothers made their presence known, Madonna's label Maverick signed another English act: the Prodigy. Under the direction and production skills of Liam Howlett, the Prodigy had been trying to connect with U.S. audiences for years, with limited suc-cess. But by moving some of its members to the forefront and exaggerat-ing its image, the group finally broke through, eventually becoming hugely successful. Electronica now had two solid pillars to build upon, giving other English groups like Underworld, Propellerheads, Portishead, and Fatboy Slim something to stand on as they made the leap to U.S. audiences.

Nearly all of these English artists, whether through natural or premed-itated processes, incorporated rock 'n' roll elements in their sound. Even simple ingredients like sampled guitar riffs were enough to anchor this "new" music to something American consumers could understand. The "breakbeat"—the building block of hip-hop—did the same. Together, guitar riffs and breakbeats connected electronica to the combination Americans already knew and loved: that of rock and hip-hop,[5] tracing back

to Run-DMC's 1986 breakthrough "Walk This Way" and Beastie Boys' records old and new.

This reliance on traditional rock band sounds is not difficult to understand—forty-odd years of rock 'n' roll have left a power-ballad patina on the music industry's minds and business practices. As Wohelski recalls, "The Chemical Brothers were coming on tour, and someone who was an artist manager on the West Coast . . . sat down with me and my partner. He thought the Chemicals were amazing and wanted them to do a remix for a group that he also managed. He said, 'They would be so much cooler if they had a drummer.'"

Missing Channels

In the rush to bring electronica to market, labels juggled integrity and artist development with hype and sales figures. And not all were as careful as

Astralwerks. Electronica became a successful and easily copied formula for marketing techno, but much was lopped off in the process.

Techno is an expression of complicated, paradoxical, and delicately balanced ideas that can't always be communicated to the masses. Like hip-hop, it represents a new way to experience, perform, and distribute music. Hip-hop was originally an interwoven culture of rapping, spinning, break-dancing, and graffiti art. The latter three were jettisoned during hip-hop's commercial ascension. Techno suffered a similar fate in gaining a popular definition, lacking hip-hop's ability to garner massive attention and success as it developed under the American microscope. Techno has had to find other avenues, from alternative distributors to the giant "invisible industry" of raves, clubs, DJs, and promoters.

But just as techno represents an antithesis to the music industry, it is also very much *of* the industry. From the remnants of Detroit's old Motown musical legacy to the *Billboard* charts, techno has plenty of untold or undiscovered American heritage that exists well within the confines of popular music, including links to disco, soul, and R&B.

Still speaking on behalf of Astralwerks at the time, Wohelski was hopeful in 1997 that techno's respect will come, compared to, say, disco. "All we can hope is that this music will be accepted as something different and marketed as such," he said. "I wouldn't market a Herbie Hancock record the way I would market a Pearl Jam record, would I? All we can hope is that it will be accepted on its own musical merit, instead of [as] this bastard stepchild . . . that it will be accepted as an honored, full-fledged member of the music industry as a genre." A decade later, as label manager, Americas, for Beatport (an online music store), Wohelski is fully aware that his hope seems to have become a reality.

> Considering the circumstances and events of the last decade, yes, I think we have reached that point. I could have never predicted that dot-com bubble would burst, Web 2.0 would carry such a powerful impact on global culture, and the music industry as we knew it would implode. Dance music and DJ culture have become more accepted in the fabric of mainstream culture. Rock bands like Linkin Park have a DJ and Motley Crüe drummer Tommy Lee tours as a DJ. The genre is represented as part of the Grammy Award panel. The development of computer-based music-making technology like Ableton Live and Propellerheads' Reason —developed by DJs—have infiltrated mainstream music production.

The proliferation of digital music and the success of digital music retailers such as iTunes and Beatport have created an environment in which there is unprecedented access to all genres of music at the click of a mouse. Social networking sites such as MySpace and Facebook and music discovery tools like Last.fm have leveled the playing field, encouraging the independent music sector and even the musicians themselves to compete with the big labels. All that's needed is to build a community and make music that resonates with people.

Looking back, it's impossible to tell if the heightened media awareness of electronica in the late 1990s got techno where it is today, or if much of this has happened covertly in its global subculture. The hope was that the music would become as assimilated into American culture as it is in every other corner of the world. The truth is a lot more complicated and remains long after the promise of the electronica marketing push has faded. Success seems to have come more through osmosis than through any one record or music video. Even the electronic music magazine *XLR8R* suggests that the concept, if not the genre itself, has outlived its usefulness: "this is where the media broke the ground for electronica's early grave—the second some know-it-all critic gave a stack of dance music niches one homogenous name."[6]

So it seems that techno's cultural assimilation in this country will be gradual after all. That in itself is fascinating—that even old-fashioned American media and marketing muscle have failed to elevate or morph it into anything approaching pop culture. More fascinating yet are techno's origins. How did it get there? And where did it come from? The fact is, techno developed outside the coastal spheres of media influence. It developed in cities *starved* for the excitement of a New York, Los Angeles, or London—in English cities like Sheffield and Manchester, and Midwestern American hubs like Chicago and Detroit. What's more, this "new" musical revolution is nearly thirty years old.

And Time Becomes a Loop

In the short timeframe between the early and mid-1980s, the world of popular music was up for grabs. The ebb of disco could still be heard and felt, and the crossover monoliths of the mid-1980s—Michael Jackson, George Michael, and Madonna—had not yet emerged to dominate the industry. In this window of musical opportunity, all manner of sounds came crashing through under the catch-all term "new wave." (Looking back, the term "electronica" seems like an inevitability.) Techno producer and former radio DJ Alan Oldham describes this period as "back when MTV wasn't dictating the style [and] when black kids weren't penalized for being into rock." It was in this open period that the somewhat austere German group Kraftwerk emerged to prominence, becoming an integral link to future styles like techno and house. As Mark Sinker and Tim Barr posited in *The History of House,* "With all eyes on the Beatles and the Rolling Stones, almost no one in the mid-1960s could have predicted that two students studying highbrow musical theory at Dusseldorf [*sic*] Conservatory would go on to unveil the future."[7]

Starting with 1974's *Autobahn,* Kraftwerk single-handedly moved electronic instrumentation out of the cloistered workspaces of inventors and theoreticians and into the bloodstream of popular music. The group's transformation from progressive rockers to purveyors of techno-pop is documented in Pascal Bussy's biography *Kraftwerk: Man, Machine and Music.* Writes Bussy, "This [*Autobahn*] once again could have put Kraftwerk back in a category with the 'conceptual rock' of Pink Floyd or King Crimson. But what made *Autobahn*'s title track unique was that it was not a classical rock symphony with parts and movements, it was in effect one very long pop song."[8]

By the time Kraftwerk recorded *Trans-Europe Express* in 1977 and *Computer World* in 1981, its meticulousness in the studio was reflected in a much-imitated straight-laced appearance and a seamless, machine-perfect sound. Clean, syncopated rhythms propelled Kraftwerk's sound into the realm of dance music, described by many American listeners as "so stiff it's funky."

The legacy of Kraftwerk's sound can be neatly traced to many more recent forms of electronic music. The group's direct influence on New York's Afrika Bambaataa and the Soulsonic Force and producer Arthur Baker,[9] for example, resulted in Bambaataa's 1982 record "Planet Rock," which exploded onto the dance scene and helped define the genre "electro" (short for "electronic funk"), changing forever the way hip-hop would be produced. But "Planet Rock" was only one single. Kraftwerk would also influence several other European and American sounds. Many Chicago house pioneers cite Kraftwerk's 1981 record "Home Computer" as an early reference point. Likewise, electro and pre-techno artists in Detroit drew inspiration from the bizarre portamento riffs and lyrical minimalism of the group's "Numbers," also released in 1981.

This connection between Detroit and Kraftwerk may seem mysterious until one looks between original members Ralf Hütter and Florian Schneider[10]—literally. On stage and on many of their album covers, group members Karl Bartos and Wolfgang Flur were placed in the middle, performing the group's electronic percussion duties. Bartos and Flur were added at separate intervals—just after the *Autobahn* and *Ralf & Florian* albums, respectively. With this dedicated rhythm section, Kraftwerk's sound took on a new dimension, bringing it closer to soul and dance music (and Detroit), and farther from musical theory.

Just as critics were beginning to understand the Beach Boys' influence on vocal harmonies in the *Autobahn* album, Kraftwerk's love of soul and dance music started to significantly work its way into the group's music. As former Kraftwerk member Karl Bartos explains, "We were all fans of American music: soul, the whole Tamla/Motown thing, and of course James Brown. We always tried to make an American rhythm feel, with a European approach to harmony and melody." This combination is audible at least as far back as "Trans-Europe Express" in 1977, but is most pronounced in the group's 1983 hit single "Tour de France." Probably Kraftwerk's most explicit and visceral emulation of a real-world object, "Tour de France" bases its rhythm around the chain, pedal, and gear sounds of bicycles. Intentionally or otherwise, the metallic gliding and ticking of these sounds recalls the tight, rhythmic guitar work of Jimmy Nolen on James Brown staples like "Cold Sweat."

With the release of "Tour de France," Kraftwerk was poised at the crest of a cultural feedback loop—its reengineered pop and soul was connecting with R&B artists who had already begun incorporating electronics. By the time *Electric Café* was released in 1986, Americans were well versed in Kraftwerk, thanks to adventurous radio programmers in tune with disco and progressive rock, and to the group's inclusion in the new wave and "neue Deutsche Welle" scenes of England and Germany. (Kraftwerk was also a primary influence for nearly all of the bands to emerge out of these two movements.)

Many historical reconstructions of techno's past name Kraftwerk and funk music as the sole influences on early techno. Perhaps it was this quote from techno pioneer Derrick May that set the precedent for this connection: "The music [techno] is just like Detroit—a complete mistake. It's like George Clinton and Kraftwerk stuck in an elevator."[11] If only May could collect royalties on this sound bite! Intended as an off-the-cuff remark, it was quickly snapped up by the European press and has been used as a text-book definition for techno ever since. But while it's true that Kraftwerk had a far-reaching effect on electronic music as a whole, this simplifica-tion ignores techno's complex range of influences, many of which came not from Germany but from the Midwestern American city of Detroit.

Children of Production

Surprisingly, Kraftwerk's sound was absorbed more easily and more com-pletely in the American Midwest than in larger metropolitan cities like New York and Los Angeles. This was especially true in Detroit, where the band's craftsmanlike pop songs perhaps served as tonic for a pervasive assembly-line aesthetic and the fallout following the 1967 riots.

Techno "happened" in Detroit—perhaps because the new musical genre needed quiet environs to grow and develop. In a larger metropolis, the danger of a fickle populace latching onto another trend the following week, or of it being burned under critics' magnifying lenses, would have kept techno from becoming the global phenomenon it is today. Detroit's precious post-industrial condition was how and where techno's nuances developed exponentially, rather than with a limiting, linear progression. By becoming an entity unto itself, techno avoided being pinned as simply an extension of Chicago house music.

Techno is also in some ways a contrary reaction to Detroit, rather than merely a sum of its influences. Within the city's African American com-munity was a generation of young adults looking to escape the legacies of Berry Gordy and George Clinton, or maybe already detecting conserva-tive and formulaic tendencies in black radio. When the time came for these kids' inevitable teenage rebellion, they turned away from R&B and looked instead to Kraftwerk and other European artists. These young techno rebels thought they had found R&B's polar opposite, when in fact they were just hearing American soul music through unfamiliar filters.

Techno was a Herculean triumph in overcoming cultural isolation and desperation and, for most of its existence, has struggled to survive in a rock 'n' roll-dominated landscape. To put it succinctly, techno was way ahead of its time, notwithstanding its antiquated notions of the future, synthesizer relics, and dystopian backdrop. Even the term "techno"—often cited as coming directly from Alvin Toffler's book *The Third Wave*—connotes a connection to future and futurism. In his book, Toffler outlines his concept of "techno rebels"—people who are cautious of new, powerful technologies and want to temper the breakneck pace of technological advancement. As he asserts, "The techno-rebels contend that technology need not be big, costly, or complex in order to be 'sophisticated.'"[12]

While Toffler's description may evoke a different image than musicians with unconventional instruments, the common ground is a simplification of technology and an emphasis on maximizing the potential of the individual. Indeed, techno's underlying philosophy has less to do with futurism, as is commonly believed, than with the power of the individual and personal visions of Utopia. Even the most "hard core" and militant-sounding techno groups, like Detroit's Underground Resistance, have lofty, Roddenberry-like ideals at heart—scenarios where race is no longer an issue.

There's just as much to be said about techno as a social phenomenon (even prior to the "rave" era) as there are theories to explain the frequencies and modulations of its waveforms. Our story will trace the routes of techno's cultural and musical "give and take" from the late 1970s and early 1980s onward, with Detroit as the major reference point, along with various happenings in the United Kingdom, Germany, and the Netherlands. Detroit may not be a "complete mistake," as May had said, but its odd circumstances and challenging environment combined to help shape the future of popular music.

2

Party Out
of Bounds

The Pre-History of
Techno, 1978–1983

Buried under both the hype and the mystery surrounding today's techno lies a simple idea: teenage kids finding escape and release in music. This seems to be a universal experience — young people, through serious interest in music and the consumer act of purchasing an album, experience their first real sense of empowerment. In the Detroit of the late 1970s and 1980s, African American youth took that notion further than anyone had imagined. The resulting scene set the stage for techno music.

Social outlets were few for teenagers in the divested Detroit of that time. Teen dance clubs that had once existed in the suburbs had vanished, and this generation wasn't big on being labeled "teens" anyway. The options that remained included school-sponsored dances, going to the movies, or, God forbid, hanging around with one's family. Simply put, Detroit was a far cry from the teenage Utopias portrayed in 1980s films like *Pretty in Pink* and John Hughes's *Ferris Bueller's Day Off*.

Compounding this generation's frustrations were lingering memories of Detroit's past glory, as well as questionable attempts at revitalization. Projects intended to regenerate downtown activity, such as the high-end Renaissance Center (a combination luxury hotel/office building complex) and an inner-city mall called "Trapper's Alley," were at best disconnected from the rest of the city. Worse was their assumed function as cultural replacements. Instead, Detroit's youth congregated in outlying shopping malls, especially Northland Mall in the suburb of Southfield. Such places may be second nature to teenage suburbanites, but these were residents of the nation's Seventh City![1] Having to downshift from metropolis to the 'burbs just to be entertained or to socialize doesn't make for a stellar sense of civic pride.

Everything Just Cliqued

Filling this cultural void would become the preoccupation of high school students in northwest Detroit,[2] who went beyond the usual high school social cliques to organize a more formalized approach to dances and parties—Detroit's "party clubs." These predominantly male social clubs were focused almost exclusively on organizing parties. Crews of young club members booked DJs, arranged for lights and equipment, and rented space to provide something between homespun backyard parties and professional DJ services.

Perhaps as a result of clique dynamics, a need to distance themselves from negative stereotypes, or simply the class division existing between the northwest side and the rest of the city, Detroit's high school social clubs took on elitist characteristics. Some were more exclusive than others, but all centered on somewhat naïve ideas of sophistication, class, and distinction. Apart from some adjunct girls' groups in their later days, the clubs were all male, and their defining concepts and styles were culled from upscale clothiers and magazines such as *Gentleman's Quarterly* and *L'Uomo*

Vogue. Appropriately, the original four clubs were named Plush, Funtime Society, Universal, and GQ Productions.

Generally speaking, the club motif was a continuum from classic 1980s "preppy" to genuine and knock-off European labels. Hassan Nurullah, a Detroit high school student at the time, distinctly remembers the era's staples: "For a while, everyone was wearing Max Julien jackets, Roots sidewinders [a leather boot that laces up the side], and those double-breasted shirts. We used to emphasize the shoes more—you had to have at least four or five pairs of Roots to be considered cool." Nurullah also remembers some of the era's stranger new wave fashions.

> I remember Mike Bonner and I were at Northland [Mall] when the B-52's first album came out. We saw this bright-ass yellow record and weird-looking people singing weirder songs: "There's a moon in the sky and it's called the moon." "What is this weird crap?" we laughed. But soon we were out buying Hawaiian shirts, bright yellow cargo pants, wild sunglasses, Fiorucci "safety" jeans, and Kansai Yamamoto T-shirts—the brightest, most obnoxious stuff.

The low-end American brands might have been what the majority could afford, but the kids got much more mileage out of the unattainable. Nearly half of the clubs named themselves after Italian stores or designers, or made up similar-sounding names: Giavante, Ciabittino,[3] Schiaparelli, Remnique, Courtier, Cacharel, Arpegghio, Avanté, and so on. At times, reading a club's party flyer sounded more like name-dropping and gossiping beside Milanese and Parisian runways than it did cafeteria and hallway chatter in Detroit.

More impressive than the brand-name threads they wore, however, was the way in which these kids essentially created their own nightlife: plugging into the city's network of clubs and halls and quickly migrating out of parents' and grandparents' backyards. In fact, some of the clubs' self-styled promoters began organizing parties before they could even transport themselves to the venues. Promoter Kevin Bledsoe remembers: "The first party I ever gave was in the tenth grade, at the Chin Tiki [a supper club that sometimes rented space]. My mother drove me. She dropped me off [and then] came back and picked me up at 2:00 A.M. She didn't know it [the party] ended at 2:00 [A.M.] —I didn't tell her that. She was sitting outside from 12:30 to 2:00, mad as I don't know what, but she couldn't believe how many kids were up in there."

Bledsoe, who initially threw parties for the club Fifth Avenue New York, later formed the legendary Charivari club with his brother Brian and a few friends. Charivari took its name from a small chain of hip clothing stores in New York City that Bledsoe had visited while attending the Fashion Institute of Technology the summer after graduating from high school. *Charivari* is an antiquated French word meaning "hullabaloo," but it was simply the sound of the word and its association with the store that mattered to the club and its members.

By the time Charivari began attracting a following in 1980, there were several players in the high school party game—two or three clubs per school, and multiple parties every weekend. This didn't go unnoticed by Todd Johnson, another young Detroiter, who had already supplied a few Charivari parties with sound, lights, and DJs via his booming business Direct Drive.[4] "They introduced me to the whole thing," said Johnson. "[Charivari] didn't know they had a gold mine on their hands . . . they were just the wild boys, the playboys." Johnson was the one who gave Charivari their catchy tag line: "Our parties keep you together while you let yourself go."

One venue for the parties of Charivari and other social clubs was the third floor of the Women's City Club, a counterpart to the Detroit Athletic Club and sometime meeting place of women's activist groups since the 1920s. This third-floor space became known as the Park Avenue Club, named for the building's location on Park Avenue, directly behind the Fox Theater (a vestige of the golden age of movie palaces).

The six-story Women's City Club housed a variety of music scenes on any given night, and its status as an institution explains a lot about both the scarcity of Detroit nightlife in the early 1980s and the tendency for nightlife-driven talent to cluster in the oddest urban locales. While there was next to nothing going on throughout most of the downtown area (especially along the perimeter of the then decaying theater district), the area around the Women's City Club was a microcosm of music scenes past, present, and future. Chris Jaszczak was the building's manager at the time, witnessing this gloriously odd convergence every week.

[A Charivari party] would be . . . on the third floor . . . and there'd be all these kids dancing their buns off. On the second floor there'd be [groups like] A Flock of Seagulls. And on the first floor we had the Detroit Jazz Center—old Detroiters down there listening to Sam Sanders, Bill McKinney, Roy Brooks, [and so on].

[Budding talent like] James Carter and Geri Allen were taking classes there . . . Marcus Belgrave was teaching . . . a lot of stuff was going on, all at the same time. It was a great building.

Although the Women's City Club afforded the different crowds three separate entrances, there was a fair amount of intermingling: high school kids wandered down to check out the older, white punk scene, as well as to try their luck at being served at the bar. As Jaszczak points out, all-night parties with racially mixed crowds, which are hard to find even today, are reflective of a city's creative soul—the so-called countercul-ture that is perpetually rediscovered and reinvented by forward-think-ing youth. "That's always the crowd that I've shot for 'cause I'm part of it," he says. "You get into the labels—maybe more cosmopolitan, a little more urbane. The scenes may change but the attitude never does. There's always that crowd that uses their heads for more than just separating their ears."

Separating the men from the boys in the social clubs would be the young promoters, who had trained their minds on the business aspect of these parties early on. The average party drew about 400–500 people, and the bigger players drew 800–1,200. With admission fees ranging from one to twenty dollars, these kids and young adults were making a lot of money. It's a testament to their planning and maturity that they were able to rein in their young egos—even for the duration of one party. Says Bledsoe, "The party thing just blew up and everybody was getting over. We were shopping in the Woodward Shop at Hudson's in North-land. We even had our own salesman. My father was like, 'I don't even shop there!'"

One particular Charivari party, held in the Park Avenue Club on Christmas night 1980, inspired Todd Johnson to start a social club of his own—the meticulously planned club Gables.[5] Named after Clark Gable, the club evoked an American icon of sophistication rather than the Eu-ropean leanings of other clubs. The distinct big-eared visage appeared on many a flyer, alongside the challenge, "If you miss our parties, frankly, you don't give a damn." But Johnson was masterminding on a much larger scale than those still in high school (he had graduated a few years earlier), and his plans for a super-club quickly grew into designs on cornering the market. As he recalls:

I wanted to control everything and tighten it up. [We were going to] special-
ize: GOG—Gentleman of the Galaxy—would have the jitterbug parties.
Rafael would throw the cool people's parties. Remnique would throw the GQ
[*Gentleman's Quarterly*] parties. [Gables would] throw the big huge parties, and
Charivari would throw the wild, "get loose" parties. I had it all divided and
broken down: we had all the DJs, all the equipment . . . a universal club. So if
anyone got wise, we'd all come together and throw one massive party on the
same night. We wanted to choke the industry and get paid.

Johnson's scheme fell apart at a meeting with the other clubs, whose
members figured that he was trying to take over, like some kind of preppy
czar. Says Johnson, "Something clicked for a few of them and they said,
'Oh, you're trying to run everything.' And most of 'em walked. The funny
thing was that those that walked ended up joining together! They did exactly what I had said, but instead they became my rivals." Which is not to
say that Gables itself wasn't successful. Johnson's lighting, sound, and DJ
services were already well entrenched and well oiled, making it hard to
compete with his brand of vertical integration. Those who tried usually
ended up having to go through Johnson in some capacity.

This tendency of high school kids and young adults to center their world
around parties may seem logical in any city, but the amount of risk and
responsibility assumed by this generation of Detroit youth places it in
another category—in league with Berlin's Swing Kids and the nightclub
clientele of Harlem's Renaissance. Says Nurullah, "There were no adults.
Whatever problems there were, we handled them. You can go to any city
you want and you'll never find a phenomenon like that."

In the midst of the fervor surrounding dress, music, and having a good
time, the social clubs encouraged a definite component of elitism. It was in-
nocent role-playing at its best, and exclusionary at its worst. Typical of high
school kids, the cliques and clubs were as much about divisiveness as they
were about banding together. Couple this with a middle-class upbringing
and affluent northwest Detroit base and you had a potential problem.

Two-Party System

As in any large metropolitan area, barriers both real and artificial define
Detroit's social strata. Divisions of class run parallel to those of geography,
and sometimes overlap and conflict with one another. In the early 1980s,

one such division was that between the "preps" and the "jits." "Prep" was an obvious abbreviation for "preppy," a term that doesn't have the same resonance in today's society. The preps were basically the kids in the social clubs and those attending their parties, most coming from upper-middle-class neighborhoods in northwest Detroit. The "jits" were the hip, "streetified" kids, and were generally less affluent than the preps. "Jit" was also the name of a frenetic dance, presumably descended from the 1930s jitterbug. In the context of Detroit's African American community, the two terms were analogous to the intraracial class conflicts between the "wannabes" and "jigaboos" of Spike Lee's *School Daze* and the "socs" and "greasers" in S. E. Hinton's *The Outsiders*. "Jit" remains in use today, although it is more often used in reference to the dance than to a group of people.

This schism between the preps and the jits has a lot to do with Detroit's history, and with one road in particular. Woodward Avenue, the world's first mile of concrete roadway, defines "east side" and "west side" for Detroit and the communities along its twenty-seven-mile stretch to the northern suburb of Pontiac. The early social club scene, organized by high school kids in the northwestern part of the city, was oriented exclusively toward preps. If there was concern about the "wrong" element getting into a party, a club would distribute party flyers that gave cues as to who the "expected" crowd was. "No hats and no canes" was one common phrase that translated simply into "no jits and no thugs," as canes were (and still are in some circles) an accessory and totem of gang members.

But while some see the elitism of the party scene as a result of pointed exclusionary policies, others trace it to voluntary group identification, an odd parallel to the elective tribalism of the rave phenomenon. Johnson describes the era's divisiveness as more of a mind-set.

[Since] the parties consisted mainly of the northwest Detroit crowd, some of the other people would say, "Oh, Cass Tech kids are snobs or Henry Ford people think they have money."[6] But everyone was just out trying to have fun. It wasn't so tight, but that's how everyone thought it was, so they took themselves out of it. [It's] a mental thing more than . . . a geographical thing: you decide what group you're in. People separate themselves.

Given how disconnected this generation was with its own city, the importance of self-identification makes a lot of sense. As Detroit became increasingly deemphasized in favor of the suburbs, the east-west and prep-jit divisions started losing significance. Once outside the city, attitude may have played a much larger role than geography or economics. Detroit was left as a mere locale, a backdrop for different subcultures to either run their courses or blossom into larger movements.

As the northwest party crowd aged in 1982 and 1983, its events began taking on larger dimensions and the preps' elitist airs began to disintegrate. "[The clubs] started blending as people got older and started driving," Johnson points out. "With cars, Detroit all of a sudden becomes a big place." Even though the preps had higher professional ambitions than their jit counterparts, they had been stuck in stagnant social patterns of their own design. Ironically, it would take east-side nightclubs to help broaden the preps' horizons.

East-side parties and clubs were generally rowdier and funkier, if less organized, than those of the northwestern preps. The east side also carried the torch for the early electro-funk sound (later popularized by New York's Afrika Bambaataa and the Soulsonic Force), gradually building its own scene and spreading its influence.[7] Most important, the east side was more inclusive of Detroit's youth than the west side. While parties held by west-side clubs, like the Park Avenue Club, mingled preps, punks, and jazzbos, east-side clubs like Climax and Club UBQ drew a more eclectic crowd from all areas of the city. At first, UBQ was a bit of an anomaly, as it tried to uphold the same level of exclusivity as the west-side clubs. As Keith Tucker, an east-side native and electro and techno producer, explains, "[UBQ] was trying to be a sort of elite kind of club. What they tried to do was make it upscale, and it seemed like that just didn't work. . . . It was a nice-looking place and they handled their stuff professionally . . . but it was in a bad neighborhood—Harper over near Van Dyke. As long as I can remember, that area has always been bad."

As the scope of the party domain widened, the crowds got less and less formal, and the parties themselves became faster, hotter, and sweatier—a definite contrast to the level of professionalism the club promoters had attained. "People had to sweat," Johnson remembers. "It used to be that parties were *cool*—you'd have your shirt tucked in at the beginning of the party, and it would stay tucked. Our crowd brought in the T-shirt and the pullovers, because you couldn't be cool with your shirt hanging out and your belt too tight and stuff. You came into a party to party . . . like it's supposed to be."

AN EARLY 1980S PARTY CROWD AT THE PARK AVENUE CLUB, SOMETIME BETWEEN THE "DRESS TO IMPRESS" AND "DRESS TO SWEAT" ERAS. (Todd Johnson)

Even though the protocol had been strictly preppy when it began, Johnson's club Gables seemed to be one step ahead in terms of gauging social transformations. Just as 1980s society started to dress down, with blue jean and tennis shoe companies in full swing, the coded phrase on Gables's party flyers shifted from "dress to impress" to "dress to sweat." For one small instant, the preps and jits realized that they could all get along and let music and dancing be the only thing that mattered. The preps loosened their skinny ties, and the jits realized that there were actually energetic parties out there where the only ammunition belonged to the DJ. Says one anonymous "jit" from that era: "For us, going to a party [had] meant a shoot-out or getting into a fight—it was part of the territory."

By the end of 1983, however, the mixed crowds were leading to escalating violence, and it didn't take long for things to fall apart. As Johnson explains:

You used to see just straight fisticuffs—some guys who had a beef with one another. You *might* see someone bleeding. But when people started shooting, started killing people in the party scene. . . . You have to remember, parents were still monitoring this stuff. You let them read the paper and learn there's been a shooting where they were to pick up their daughter. Do you think they're going to [let her go to] the next party?

Outside of those organizing club events, few in the 1980s party crowd recognized the scene's significance and how much they accomplished before violence overtook the city. Even the clubs' promoters have mixed memories, finding that their efforts to bring people together sometimes had more negative than positive results. Johnson explains:

[The party scene] brought the crowds together momentarily. It was a brief mix. I don't think it lasted more than a year before violence came in. And it [the violence] came in fast. When you try to expand the boundaries, when you mix volatile situations, you're going to have violence. That destroys the party scene every time. The elusive crowd that everybody's chasing starts disappearing— it's not *cool* to get socked in the eye or shot at.

From Here to Eternity
Just as Detroit's high school kids of the early 1980s didn't sit around complaining about having nowhere to go on weekends, neither were they content to compromise the freedom they had in music. These kids recognized how important good programming was, not only to themselves but to the city in general, and some even lobbied radio stations in an attempt to preserve a diverse radio spectrum. This willingness to make challenging stylistic choices is key to the creativity and energy of techno's formative years. Before the psyche of Detroit became defined by incidents or avoidance of violence—and before the "gangsta" and "ghetto superstar" music of the early and late 1990s sold cartoonish reflections of urban life back to the populace—the city was still open to sounds that didn't overtly reflect this condition. This combination of the city's access to new sounds and the kids' willingness to fight for them opened the way for Detroit's acceptance of Eurodisco, a child of the 1970s disco movement and a precursor to techno.

One of the least documented periods in dance music, if not contemporary music in general, is that following the disco "fallout" of the late 1970s. By 1980, disco backlash had reached massive proportions throughout the United States, with the exception of metropolitan New York (where

discos kept drawing crowds until well into the 1980s). The Midwest suddenly turned into a hostile environment for dance music, bounded by the
burning of disco records at Chicago's Comiskey Park and rock station
WRIF's issuance of DREAD cards to its listeners.[8]

Whether you believe disco burned itself out or was forced out of mainstream acceptance by an album rock hegemony, the music did "die" in a
commercial sense. Its followers, however, were determined to at least keep
the music's creative energies alive. In order to survive, disco had to either
become an "underground" phenomenon or maintain a camouflaged
mainstream existence. In both the United States and Europe, disco progressed down both of these avenues, but it was the latter that would yield
unpredictable results.

Disco's continued evolution remained largely hidden from the mainstream, perhaps because the records emanated from unlikely sources such
as Italy, France, and Belgium, or simply because the gay community comprised the largest segment of its audience. The resulting subgenre, which
encompassed a wide spectrum of sounds (including hi-NRG),[9] was sum-
marized as "Eurodisco," and techno and house owe as much to its electronic
upgrade of traditional disco as they do to the rhythms of Kraftwerk.

Eurodisco emerged between the late and postdisco years of 1977 and 1983,
when many European nations were rebuilding their indigenous pop scenes,
some of which had lain dormant for decades following World War II. One
of the most prolific countries during this period was Italy; its unique strain
of disco had a tremendous impact on underground dance music in the
United States. "Italo-disco" picked up where acclaimed Italian disco producer Giorgio Moroder had left off in the mid-1970s — in a rejection of
traditional instrumentation for newer electronic forms.

Born in Ortisei, Italy, Moroder was one of the first people to own a Moog
3 synthesizer, which cost upward of $10,000 when first released. Accessing
new sounds was obviously more important to Moroder than the price tag,
and he wasted no time incorporating the early synthesizer into his music;
as early as 1972 he scored a hit in Britain with "Son of My Father." By 1975,
he and colleague Pete Bellotte were using electronics to turn ordinary
dance floor numbers into sweeping, sensual epics, like the seventeen-
minute span of Donna Summer's "Love to Love You Baby." His film scores
and compositions for Donna Summer ensured that disco would not be the
one-dimensional craze of *Saturday Night Fever* or "The Hustle." Unfor-

tunately, Moroder's creative vision wasn't enough to stay the execution, as electronic instrumentation nearly died with disco. Along with the African American, Latino, and gay components of the music, the mainstream shunned synthesizers in favor of a calculated return to "traditional" rock 'n' roll and stadium-caliber concert tours.

In the late 1970s, the up-and-coming Italian producers who returned to Moroder's legacy lacked the resources and attention he had enjoyed during disco's prime, nor did they have the benefit of Munich's active club scene. (Moroder had moved to Munich in his late twenties.) So, just as their Detroit techno counterparts would do years later, the creators of Italo-disco centered their attention on more affordable and accessible technology—experimentation with sound and effects, processed vocals, and a love for the synthesizer.

The first few years of the 1980s provided this new wave of producers with audiences still receptive to the four-count beat of disco. Italo-disco also benefited from trade restrictions that had made it nearly impossible to get imports in the United States before 1980. When this restriction was lifted, American DJs and audiences starving for new dance sounds devoured the "new" Italo-disco records (some of which were two or three years old by the time Americans heard them). Dozens of influential recordings were released under the various aliases of a few talented producers: Jacques Fred Petrus was behind "Fire Night Dance" by the Peter Jacques Band and "I'm a Man" by Macho, while Easy Going's "Fear," Vivian Vee's "Give Me a Break," and the music of Capricorn masked the production talents of Italian producer Claudio Simonetti. This type of anonymity remains a hallmark of modern electronic dance music, in which the number of artist pseudonyms has risen exponentially—well into the teens for some producers.

Like Moroder, Claudio Simonetti was influential on film scores and soundtracks of the late 1970s, tracing back to his progressive rock roots with the band Goblin. Simonetti contributed music to a number of horror films, including George Romero's *Dawn of the Dead* and the Italian classic *Suspiria*,[10] both with the band and as a solo artist. An entirely different kind of horror was the Italian "cadet meets private-school girl" film *College*; an EP (extended-play record) of Simonetti's contributions to the film's soundtrack was released independently and became a hit on the pre-house dance floors of Chicago.

With a name that brings to mind Russian Kraftwerk disciples, Alexander Robotnick was another Italo-disco favorite—a pseudonym taken on by Italian Maurizio Dami of the dance-cabaret band Avida. In the early 1980s, Robotnick hit it big in Detroit with "Problèmes D'Amour," complete with French lyrics.[11] "Problèmes" was also one of the first records to feature the Roland TB-303 synthesizer, with its quirky onboard sequencer. The "303" is ubiquitous these days, a staple on countless techno and acid house records. Long before producers discovered the power of modulating bassline wave-forms in real time, Dami used it in its "intended" fashion—simply mimicking the square waves that emanate from bass guitars. The rhythm, the bassline, and the lovelorn cries of "aua" in the chorus all made "Problèmes D'Amour" one of the most hypnotic tracks of its time.

Also from Italy was Kano, the partnership of Stefano Pulga and Luciano Ninzatti. Their self-titled EP featured "It's a War," one of *Billboard*'s top ten dance hits of 1980 and a Detroit favorite. The group's follow-up single, "I'm Ready," would become one of Detroit's most revered dance cuts, as would its perfectly matched B-side, "Holly Dolly."

A more multinational import was Liaisons Dangereuses, a Belgian band with a French name that titled most of its songs in Spanish ("Los Niños del Parque" was Detroit's favorite). Perhaps this group's pan-European outlook was an extension of Kraftwerk's "Trans-Europe Express"—a song that predicted the emergence of an interconnected European continent by the end of the twentieth century. Other major influences on Detroit's sound in particular came from the likes of Klein & MBO ("Dirty Talk"), the kitschy Belgian trio Telex ("Moskow Diskow"), and French artist Martin Circus ("Disco Circus").

Parisian Jean-Marc Cerrone was second only to Moroder in terms of stature and influence among Eurodisco's pioneers. He continued evolving the disco sound after Moroder had moved on to film projects and collaborations with rock artists in the 1980s. Some experts point to Cerrone's 1976 single "Love in C Minor" as the first recording to sever all ties with traditional musical conventions. "It wasn't a *song*," says Elorious Cain of Ottawa-based ABM Records. "Up until that point there was a tremendous concentration on making songs out of disco." Cain holds that "Love in C Minor" was the start of "conceptual disco," from which house, techno, and myriad other styles would flow.

In Detroit, Italo-disco would be known simply as "progressive," which aptly described the generation's attitude toward music as well. These African American kids weren't content to limit themselves to the R&B and "urban contemporary" records being marketed to them; just as much, if not more, of their listening was produced by the mainly white artists of Eurodisco. These records became the most popular music of the high school set, bridging the gap between Detroit's east and west sides. The electronic sound that was so integral to Eurodisco found a perfect complement in the updated funk and R&B of Shannon ("Let the Music Play") and of George Clinton's solo excursions.

Another way to look at Italo-disco is as a missing link between disco and what most refer to as "new wave." This term tends to evoke a specific style and look, but it actually conceals about a dozen variants of music that grew out of late 1970s movements, including punk, synth-pop (and its "new romantic" variant), goth, ska, rockabilly, and power-pop. The migration of listeners from disco to Italo-disco to new wave spread throughout the Midwest, with Chicago acting as chief importer for the other cities—a portal through which all manner of musical oddities passed.

Just as Italo-disco had, new wave caught on with African American audiences in Detroit like nowhere else in the United States. One could hear new wave's offbeat and eclectic ingredients working themselves out in Detroit's early electronic dance records, where groups like the Human League, the B-52's, and Visage were reconciled with Eurodisco, the Midwestern funk of George Clinton, Zapp, the Ohio Players, and, subconsciously, the soul of Motown. Detroit's preps connected with the style-conscious synth-pop bands, which had exterior styles as well polished as their sound; a subset of synth-pop—the "new romantics"—even bordered on foppish, such as the group Visage. "Fade to Grey" was Visage's biggest hit, but it was the flip side that captured the Motor City's attention. Simply titled "Frequency 7," it was a surprisingly aggressive and swaggering instrumental, especially considering the new romantics' predilection for dramatic vocals and delicate melodies. Perhaps it was the influence of former Magazine member and future Bad Seed Barry Adamson that pushed their sound in this direction.

In addition to the well-known Depeche Mode, one of the few new wave bands to have smooth continuity into the 1990s, Detroit was also receptive to Japan's Yellow Magic Orchestra (Yukihiro Takahashi, Haruomi Hosono, and Ryuichi Sakamoto). YMO served as a more playful and purposefully contemporary analog to Kraftwerk, reacting to and incorporating more influences than the Düsseldorf group. Fuller arrangements, Beatles and Martin Denny covers ("Day Tripper" and "Firecracker"), and even an electronic ska song ("Multiplies") were among YMO's eclectic arsenal. In retrospect, its most interesting contribution may be the song "Technopolis," a tribute to Tokyo as an electronic mecca, foreshadowing the concepts that Detroit natives Juan Atkins and Rik Davis would later have with the group Cybotron.

Also contributing to the new wave mix were a trio of bands from Sheffield, the British steel capital: ABC, Heaven 17, and the Human League. Looking for an antidote to harsh industrial surroundings and economic hardship, these bands adopted a mock sophistication that directly influenced Detroit's high school social clubs, thereby indirectly influencing techno. One doesn't have to go much further than their album titles to see the similarity to Charivari and Ciabittino: *Penthouse and Pavement, The Luxury Gap, Beauty Stab,* and so on—all exponents of the escapism that would come to dominate the "greed is good" era.

This is where author Jon Savage's notion of "double refraction" becomes essential to understanding the sometimes nonlinear evolution of dance music. "Double refraction" refers to the process by which music is passed and copied back and forth between cultures. In his book *England's Dreaming: Anarchy, Sex Pistols, Punk Rock and Beyond,* Savage writes of England's pub bands in the 1970s: "Most of these groups were copying white British pop groups—like the Rolling Stones or the Yardbirds—that were themselves trying to capture the spirit of black American R&B."[12] By the same token, while it may seem strange that Detroit's African American teenagers were listening to the angular, almost robotic disco and soul from Europe, the European groups they idolized were themselves reflections of American music.

This exchange of musical ideas back and forth across the Atlantic has been taking place since the 1950s. Europe and the United States have developed a permanent reciprocal link, with one component merely a variation on the "grass is always greener" ideal, and another having to do with real connections between people, communicated through music. By the 1980s, Detroit was serving as a crossroads for such connections, allowing for a constant exchange of musical influence between the United States and the world.

The Beginning

It didn't take long for Detroit to reconcile and externalize all of the sensory input it was receiving from Europe, and in 1981, two recordings by Detroit artists introduced the earliest beginnings of techno as its own style and genre: "Sharevari," by A Number of Names, and "Alleys of Your Mind," by Cybotron. There's some debate as to which record actually hit the street first, but for now discussion of "Sharevari" is more pertinent as the song was both a direct extension of Italo-disco and a tribute to Detroit's high school party scene.

At the same 1980 Charivari party that inspired Todd Johnson to start the club Gables, a then unnamed group of energetic musicians brought an early demo version of a song called "Sharevari" for DJ Darryl Shannon to play. (They had changed the song's spelling to placate Brian Bledsoe, co-founder of Charivari, and to avoid potential conflicts with the Charivari clothing store chain.) Shannon started playing the record and, whether because of the song's familiar Italo-disco sound or stripped-down brand of the same, the crowd went wild, dancing to its own tailor-made anthem. "It was hitting," Kevin Bledsoe remembers. "Darryl Shannon played Kraft-werk's 'Robots' right behind it and then he dropped Quartz's 'Beyond the Clouds'—by then they [the people at the party] were up dancing on the windowsills! This was [the] first night anything like that happened. I was wondering, 'What the hell is going on?'"

According to Bledsoe, legendary radio jock Charles Johnson, also known as "the Electrifying Mojo" (or simply "Mojo"), was in the crowd that night, most likely scoping out new records popular among the high school kids. He heard "Sharevari" and convinced A Number of Names to come down to his show on radio station WGPR. Though there were only three writers credited on the record (Paul Lesley, Sterling Jones, and Roderick Simpson), a virtual army of band members showed up at the station and clogged the DJ booth. "They said, 'What do we call ourselves? We don't have a name,'" recalls Mojo. "I said, 'How many of you are there? Quite a few—why don't you call yourselves A Number of Names?' I played the record and people went crazy over it. They [A Number of Names] actually were pushing a different song ['Skitso'], but I said, '"Sharevari" is the one I'm going to play.'"

As for the musical inspiration behind "Sharevari," one doesn't have to look any further than one of the staples of the high school scene: Detroit

DJs would work two copies of Kano's "Holly Dolly," repeating the sparse intro over and over again and doubling up on the chorus of "Holly . . . Dolly." A Number of Names mimicked this interpretation of the Italo-disco classic, building on the raw rhythm track (mostly a pronounced hand clap) and the female vocal as it would sound coming from two alternating copies of the same record: "Chari Chari . . . Vari Vari." The connection between Italo-disco, techno, and Detroit's high school sophisticates can all be heard in this one single.[13]

Just as Detroit's eclectic tastes were distilled into songs such as "Sharevari," there was at least one band that was equally representative. Donald Fagenson and David Weiss were childhood friends whose penchant for drama, humor, and generally wreaking havoc in the Detroit suburb of Oak Park eventually coalesced into musical mischief as the group Was (Not Was). The duo's first single, "Wheel Me Out" (released in 1980 on Ze Records), was a rich blend of rock, funk, and jazz that connected with local and foreign audiences alike. The song was a hit of sorts in Britain and became the unofficial theme song for Todd Johnson and his Direct Drive DJs.

The band's transatlantic success led to a distribution deal with Island Records for its self-titled debut album *Was (Not Was)* in 1981. The album featured a host of young Detroit talent, among them future jazz great Marcus Belgrave on trumpet and flügelhorn. Weiss (aka David Was) and Fagenson (aka Don Was) did their part to continue the disco bloodline with the standout cuts "Out Come the Freaks" and "Tell Me That I'm Dreaming," and began to perfect the balance between Fagenson's faithful yet quirky funk and Weiss's heartfelt, satirical lyrics.

Was (Not Was) got the "brothers" noticed by emerging media magnate David Geffen, for whom they recorded their follow-up album: 1983's *Born to Laugh at Tornadoes.* This album seemed like a big-budget high school prank, as if they were asking, "I wonder how much we can get away with?" What they pulled off was an amazing contemporary funk record that incorporated more and more electronics (Oberheim OBX, Arp, and Moog synthesizers, Linn drums, and vocoders), not to mention one of the most bizarre assortments of guest vocalists in modern music. For starters, there was Mel Tormé crooning on "Zaz Turned Blue," Mitch Ryder barking on "Bow Wow Wow Wow," and Ozzy Osbourne *rapping* on "Shake Your Head (Let's Go to Bed)." All of this playful experimentation didn't help audiences or critics understand what was going on—and that suited the brothers Was just fine.[14]

It would be another five years before Was (Not Was) would become a nationally recognized name—around the time it released the single "Walk the Dinosaur" in 1988. In the interim, Fagenson began his career as a producer in earnest, working with artists such as Carly Simon. When his surrealistic side beckoned, Fagenson crafted some of the biggest local dance hits of the era. "The Beat Goes On" was released under the pseudonym Orbit, and was essentially Fagenson's answer to Kraftwerk's "Tour de France," boldly built around an old Sonny and Cher hit, of all things. Nearly all the synthesizer work on that record came from another Was (Not Was) member—a young Luis Resto, who later collaborated with Eminem and won a Best Song Oscar for "Lose Yourself" in 2003. Detroiters will also remember the early vocal/rap duo Felix and Jarvis who—with Fagenson's assistance—recorded everything from the rapid-fire new wave "Make It Rise" to the bouncy funk of "Jam the House" and "Flamethrower Rap."[15] Fagenson has since lent his talents to such high-profile projects as Bob Dylan's *Under the Red Sky,* Bonnie Raitt's *Nick of Time,* the original score to the film *Backbeat,* and the Rolling Stones' *Bridges to Babylon.* Techno owes a great debt to Fagenson and Was (Not Was). Their talent in making the paradoxical work gave the Detroit sound its edge and eventually set it apart from disco and Chicago house.

City on the Edge of Forever

The blueprint for Detroit's techno subculture ended up being as inclusive as the sound itself (although it remained a hierarchical system, with party-goers on the bottom). An extension of an already diverse music scene, it later collided with other subcultures as the high school kids grew into adults. Techno's full potential would be gradually realized as the central personalities of party promoter and DJ were transposed. DJs became recognized more for their "art" than for their practical skills, and began to draw crowds independent of whatever club or clique was sponsoring the party.

Through a sort of social osmosis, the crowds in east and west Detroit started coming together again in the mid-1980s, first in east-side clubs and eventually back downtown as they got progressively more diverse and musically adventurous. They migrated to clubs like the Liedernacht, located inside the old Leland Hotel. A number of clubs passed through this area, attracting mixed crowds of black, white, straight, and gay patrons. In a sense, this was where people who had come to techno early in its development—either in high school or on the radio—mingled in real time.

One man who could take credit for creating such a tight-knit nightlife was the late Ken Collier,[16] a legendary DJ who had perfected his craft during the disco era. Collier's contribution to Detroit's club scenes, to the development of its DJ talent, and to the early evolution of techno is immeasurable. He became a father figure to the generation of high school partygoers in the early 1980s, as well as to Detroit's gay community right up until his untimely death in 1996. Collier played through decades of parties and clubs, using his knack for knowing exactly what to play to transform simple nights out into religious experiences.

Collier was just beginning to get the worldwide respect he deserved—playing the gigantic Mayday festival in Berlin—when he fell prey to a late-diagnosed diabetic condition. Following his death in 1996, there were several efforts to preserve his memory, including a tribute album on Intangible Records and a terse eulogy penned by Alan Oldham and posted on the Internet, excerpted below.[17]

> Ken was the first person to champion Detroit techno. He and his brother Greg spun the first techno records ["Strings of Life," "No UFOs," etc.] at the club Todd's, a dance music mecca that exposed the masses to new music [punk, new wave, industrial, and house on alternate nights]. After Todd's closed, Ken held sway at Heaven, a second-floor club that's not a mile from where I live. His "children" lived to hear him play week after week.
>
> He also was a resident at Times Square, a downtown club where his "children" followed him after Heaven burned down. He was a great champion of our music, in the great black music tradition. When it was black and gay, before it became fashionable and suburban.

Other fans recall Collier's incredible skill and somewhat flamboyant demeanor behind the turntables. "He was awesome," remembers Hassan Nurullah. "He'd get that big booty going, have a little glass of cognac . . . and he didn't do anything fancy, he just had a sense of what worked. He would keep the party booming the whole time."

Like many young DJs of their time, high school friends Juan Atkins and Derrick May were inspired by Collier, learning directly and indirectly from

DJ KEN COLLIER SCHOOLS A YOUNG DETROIT CROWD IN 1981. (Todd Johnson)

him. Atkins and May formed an outsider DJ collective known as Deep Space, making a small but recognizable dent in the party system dominated by Gables and Charivari. The impact of Deep Space was limited in part by geographical distance—both Atkins and May had moved out of Detroit with their families to Belleville, a small city twenty-five miles to the southwest, making it next to impossible to get to the forefront of the party scene. Says Gables's Nurullah, "In those days, we didn't think much of Deep Space. They were never really the competition. They'd have the parties that we were too booked up to handle."

Indeed, the real opportunities for Atkins and May would come later, as they eventually became two of techno's most influential pioneers. "All those so-called snob parties, playing for all those kids and organizations—for us it was dress rehearsal," says May. "Even though we were young, we had serious dedication for what we were doing. That's why Juan [Atkins] called it Deep Space. We always saw ourselves as being 'out there.'" Perhaps sensing the potential of "conceptual disco," Atkins had been outlining his musical ideas since high school. In addition to Deep Space, May remembers him planning other projects: "He [Atkins] was talking about Metroplex back when we were seventeen years old. He said, 'I'm going to make a label one day and I'm going to call it Metroplex Records.' But I don't believe that we were as far ahead as people want to make us believe. I think we were just being young—visionaries that didn't want to be like everybody else."

May's activities included his clique KAOS,[18] which was separate from and less established than Deep Space. Named for espionage operatives on the TV show *Get Smart*, KAOS was formed by May and friend Victor Littlejohn, who painted the group's army jackets (most of the other clubs sported baseball-style satin jackets) and paraphernalia. May recalls, "We had amazing flyers back then, [which contained] these subliminal messages of an alternative way of thinking. We were trying to attract people that wanted to be alternative and wanted to be different, but our definition of alternative was the kind of music we were making—not so much a lifestyle . . . [but] just the way you thought about music. Far too often people associate the term 'alternative' with borderline rock."

The great thing about the 1980s and the high school scene in and around Detroit was how quickly and seamlessly an interest in music or style turned into mind-sets and philosophies that encoded hopes and dreams. But if these early beginnings of techno were about freedom and escapism, it wasn't long before they were tempered by the constraints of reality. Outside the autonomous existence of the high school kids, opportunities were few for the rest of Detroit. The city hid behind a layer of dormant tension and apathy, with its cultural, economic, and social biorhythms all in ebb. This strange condition plagued Detroit's creative community throughout the decade, forcing the techno movement to linger at a grassroots level.

The Beauty of Decay

Ten years after Berry Gordy packed up Motown in 1972, Detroit was a very different city—a place where a new musical movement would be hard to spot. By the mid-1980s, Detroit's once-great music industry had been reduced to a mere vestigial organ, with a dwindling number of studios and producers. Unlike Chicago, which had a well-established theater, comedy, and music community, Detroit was left without a staging area and its new talent with few choices: fend for yourself or move to one of the coasts.

Detroit's failure as a musical and cultural capital was only part of the problem facing the city's developing techno sound. Completing the ruinous picture were economic downturns and the long-term effects of racial tension. The city was left trapped in a pattern of stagnancy. The most obvious way to trace these effects is through Detroit's "post-industrial" condition, or rather what has happened to the city since the introduction of foreign competition and the decentralization of the auto industry.

Detroit's identity and well-being were (and are) tightly bound to the production of cars and trucks. When Japanese and German automotive companies started pursuing more aggressive business tactics in the 1970s, Detroit suffered along with its automakers as it lacked the alternative industries needed to pick up the economic slack. Plant closings, relocations, and the dreaded euphemism "downsizing" all became harsh realities for American automakers, suppliers, autoworkers and their families, and the economy in general. As the auto industry lies at the core of U.S. industry, the entire country feels the strain.

The cruel irony is that while Detroit's automotive giants entered a bubble of recovery through the combination of high SUV margins and cheap gasoline, Detroit itself did not share in the turnaround. In fact, the automotive industry has continued to become less and less synonymous with Detroit, slowly moving its plants and headquarters outside the city limits. (Today, only General Motors still has its headquarters there.) Though many vital components of the auto industry are still located in the city and surrounding areas, "Detroit" now stands as a mere representation of its historical importance—a collective nameplate for the "Big Three" (General Motors, Ford, and Chrysler Group LLC).

Combine Detroit's lack of economic resilience with the fear and prejudice that lingered from the riots of 1967, and the city had a recipe for disaster. As Neil Ollivierra describes in his (unpublished) novel "Reality Slap," "When I turn onto Fisher North, the exit ramp raises me over the sleeping metropolis, speckled with lights—a false and flattering view that makes you believe, for a moment, that you're in a real city. A real city, rather than this—an abandoned industrial hell that broke ground and somehow kept on growing."[19]

Detroit's symbolic and final straw came with Motown's departure in 1972—there would be no cultural safety net, no solace in the voices of Marvin Gaye and Smokey Robinson. And while the auto industry did its rebuilding and rebounding throughout most of the 1980s, the loss of culture in Detroit has been much harder to remedy. There are no short-term stimulants or federal aid packages that can restore the lost sense of community or the metropolis that once was.

Not that Detroit didn't try. The Renaissance Center and the People Mover — two pet projects of former mayor Coleman Young — at least had kernels of good ideas. Erected in 1977, the "Ren Cen" was to become the new city center and usher in a new "renaissance" for downtown Detroit. It did neither, being too expansive for Detroit's immediate needs and too self-contained to involve a larger cross-section of communities.

Another problem that has plagued Detroit (and is perhaps as responsible for the city's problems as racial tensions or economic shifts) is that of mass transportation. With the city's old trolley system forced into obsolescence by the introduction of a bus system (vehicles manufactured and supplied by General Motors), Detroit needed a new complement to transit via the combustion engine. Addressing the fundamental problem of getting from point A to point B was the charge of the People Mover "line," set in motion in 1987. Initially, its route was supposed to extend up Woodward Avenue (one of the few stretches in the metropolitan area with frequent and reliable bus service). Having run out of funding prematurely, however, it now only circles around the core of Detroit's largely abandoned downtown — similar in some ways to Chicago's famous loop. The People Mover is now either a $200 million toy train set or an odd, three-mile-long tour of Detroit's neglected buildings juxtaposed with shiny new infusions of cash.

Throughout this period, Detroiters, who had once been citizens of a prosperous city, were somehow recast as statistics — especially in regard to the dwindling population that today stands at around nine hundred thousand. Residents who remained in Detroit were dehumanized and disempowered, as were the structures surrounding them as the city could no longer sustain the office, transportation, and shopping needs of a city one-and-a-half times its size.[20] Throughout much of the 1980s, one of the most striking scenes to witness was Detroit's modern ghost-town effect: once commuters cleared out of the downtown in the evening, one could walk for blocks without encountering another person. Tracing this effect in his book *AfterCulture: Detroit and the Humiliation of History,* Jerry Herron writes, "It wasn't only in a physical sense that people left the city. . . . Just as they had abandoned the geographic space of the great towns, they abandoned the economy of centralized dreaming (and spending) represented by its business and cultural institutions."[21]

The peculiar condition of Detroit's architecture has been well documented and reflected in the works of several local artists and organizations, ranging from preservation societies and periodicals to the infamous installation *Demolished by Neglect*. Dismantled in 1987, *Demolished* consisted of enlarged photographs of various downtown structures, each attached to the actual building with the caption "Demolished by Neglect." Public officials were outraged by the installation and reportedly tried to charge the artists with vandalism—apparently missing the irony that they had previously been unconcerned about the barrage of handbills covering the neglected buildings. Recent years have even brought Detroit's architecture to the World Wide Web: a site called "The Fabulous Ruins of Detroit" takes users on a tour of Detroit's rich architectural history.[22]

Techno's future artists and producers seemed to connect on a more personal level with Detroit's buildings than did the preservationists or guerrilla artists. The juxtaposition between their new music and ideas and this old Midwestern city would continually drive their creativity, as in this observation from techno artist Juan Atkins in 1997: "I was smack in the middle of downtown, on Griswold. I was looking at [the side of] this building and I see the faded imprint of [an] American Airlines [corporate logo], the shadow [that was left] after they took the sign down. It just brought home to me the thing about Detroit—in any other city you have a buzzing, thriving downtown."

Aware of both the city's former glory and its future possibilities, these artists found hope in a decaying infrastructure where none apparently existed. This optimism and empathy would run deep in techno music, even as early as Cybotron's 1984 classic "Techno City," on which Juan Atkins's vocals are processed to sound ancient and mysterious, echoing the old soul of Detroit, while his lyrics welcome visitors to the city.

Such sentiments would also presumably lead techno's pioneers to settle in a downtown neighborhood, rather than in the suburban comfort of their youth. Techno's rebels weren't usually overtly rebellious, but establishing a base of operations in the city center was at least a contrary gesture—they could have easily opted for the convenience of expansive industrial parks and office complexes. It's true that downtown rents were probably much cheaper for the young artists, but there was also a sense of wanting to restore some of downtown Detroit's artistic nucleus.

For residents and regular visitors to the city, perverse architectural sightings continue to be all too obvious and frequent, particularly during the period in which the downtown underwent massive restructuring to accommodate three new casinos, a new ballpark for the Detroit Tigers, and a football stadium for the Detroit Lions. Seemingly without much care for continuity or gradual evolution over the last thirty years, old is giving way to new—making real the farcical "Old Detroit/New Detroit" schism in the 1987 film *Robocop*.[23] In the film, "New Detroit" is a strictly controlled, glistening Utopia, while "Old Detroit" represents lawlessness and bleak post-industrial settings. Obviously, "Old Detroit" was Hollywood's take on the city as seen through the funhouse mirror of the news media. Techno's interpretation of Detroit, while steeped in futuristic lore, would always be more realistic and accurate than the overview presented by both national and, sadly, even local media outlets.

In *AfterCulture,* Herron blames internal forces for much of Detroit's identity crisis, citing local television stations as helping fuel wild notions held by the detached suburbs about Detroit.[24] "Instead of instancing the decentered 'technoburbs' that are now the basis of middle class life," writes Herron, "the news enacts a nightly eternal return, playing out an absentee fantasy of origins." Herron's analysis points to suburban residents who, instead of receiving real news about Detroit and their own communities, are tele-tourists on a nightly survey of the city's violence, neglect, and erosion. Many positive developments (including techno) have gone unnoticed by TV audiences, who receive their information through such narrow and biased filters.

The hyperbole continued to escalate following the bizarre ritual of Devil's Night arson that occurred across the city throughout the 1980s,[25] and the mayhem following both the Tigers' World Series championship in 1984 and the Pistons' second NBA championship in 1990. It was as if violence was all that defined Detroit; the city's notoriety as the "murder capital" still lingers, even though it is no longer statistically accurate. Detroit became a national symbol for all that was wrong with America's cities, suffering more from the negligence of the media than from any specific criminal acts.

The city's negative publicity culminated in two controversial and highly publicized works—Ze'ev Chafets's book *Devil's Night and Other True Tales of Detroit* and a segment on *ABC Primetime Live* titled "Detroit Is Burning"[26]—both as incendiary as the city's fiery October nights. Despite the protests of its citizens and an especially outraged mayor, Detroit was handed its role as urban scapegoat, becoming the grand exception to the rule of American superiority and success. As Herron states, "Detroit has to be deprived of its reality so that everyone else can feel better about theirs."

Beyond its post-industrial condition, Detroit is also victim to much older problems. As efficient as its factories are or were at any given time, the city has been inefficiently fragmented in any number of ways, ranging from transit issues to a general tendency to grow out, rather than up. And despite a diverse populace, geographical barriers and the absence of convenient mass transit have made integration and healing difficult, if not impossible. Beginning with the east-side/west-side divide along Woodward Avenue, Detroit has been compartmentalized into isolated neighborhoods, with both positive and negative effects. Neighborhoods can of course nurture families, local schools, and community involvement, but they can also turn unhealthy when residents lose the ability to think or act beyond their borders. Despite the global reach of the auto industry, there is something about Detroit that contains its collective worldview in the tangle of freeways surrounding the metropolitan area.

This attempt to be cosmopolitan while keeping a regional mind-set would become a dichotomy shared by both Detroit and techno music. Nearly all of the techno DJs and producers who emerged from Detroit still live in the city, even though their work can take them to a different city or country each weekend (or often to several countries in one trip). And for a few, even though the opportunity to travel abroad was immediately available, there was an early reluctance to leave Detroit, let alone enter into business relationships with foreign entities.

If there's one thing to be learned from examining Detroit and its musicians, it's how African American artists grew up in (and wanted to be a part of) a city that was increasingly alien to them. Detroit techno would become filled with longing voices and chords—sounds that must seem melancholy and even trite to European audiences who, by comparison, live in cities that still manage to thrive. In addition, much of techno's future popularity in Europe came out of the eu(ro)phoria associated with raves and such momentous events as the fall of the Berlin Wall, forging an association between techno and elation, rather than with more somber moods.

As Detroit's "future" actually comes to pass, following the current attempt at downtown revitalization, there may be a tendency to erase and rewrite the history contained within its old structures. Perhaps more worrisome, Detroit's new progress threatens to obscure *recent* history and smaller attempts to turn things around. As Herron describes in *AfterCulture,* "The city [Detroit] is neither one thing nor the other, neither the empty dark places nor the shiny restored ones; it is both at once, back and forth: a land of monumental gestalt puzzle."[27] It was in the midst of this continuum that Detroit techno came to life, a music that echoes the ups, downs, and uncertain times of urban America.

3

Time to
Express

Techno's First Artists
Emerge, 1981–1989

As Detroit began attracting attention for the wrong reasons in the 1980s, a more positive development was quietly taking shape in basement studios and on the local airwaves. Though violence had temporarily put an end to the network of high school parties and club promoters, interest in electronic music grew exponentially. By 1983, Detroit was primed for a new beginning. Its cultural regeneration would begin with a group of high school kids who would become techno's first artists and producers, and with a handful of innovative radio programs and one ground-breaking dance club that would help these pioneers connect with listeners.

Play It Cool

Born on December 9, 1962, in Detroit, Juan Atkins grew up with a healthy and early interest in music. "I always made music," he says. "My father bought me an electric guitar when I was ten years old." Unlike most other techno pioneers, who lived on Detroit's northwest side, Atkins lived on the east side until his parents divorced while he was in his teens. Atkins and his brother Aaron moved with their father to Belleville, where his grandmother lived, while another brother and sister stayed in Detroit with their mother. As Atkins remembers, "The decision to move out of Detroit was that I was a bad high school student. I was getting kicked out of school. . . . I think at the heart of the decision was [an effort] to get me and my brother out before it was 'too late.' The change definitely helped, although I didn't like it."

It's not hard to see why. The Atkinses were one of the few black families in the area, and Belleville was not immune to the divisive effects of the 1967 riots. In addition, the suburbs didn't have the same attractions, parties, or energy as the city. "When I first moved to Belleville, I couldn't stand it," Atkins recalls. "So every chance I got to come back to Detroit, I came. My mom was here [in Detroit], so I'd spend weekends, holidays, whatever break I had with her."

Trips back to Detroit and access to his father's car now and again were the only chances Atkins had to get away. The tighter confines of Belleville, a small community, apparently kept him in check: "There was a big yellow bus that picked me up right in front of my house, so there was no way you could go wrong," he recalls. "Then in school I said, 'I'm here so I might as well learn.'" Strangely enough, among the things Atkins learned at Belleville High School were the theories of Alvin Toffler and his peers in a "future studies" class. To the average high school student, the concepts of futurism probably aren't any more useful than the capital of South Dakota. But for a displaced city kid like Atkins, unhappy with the present, they sparked imagination and creativity.

These futuristic ideas and concepts stuck with Atkins, probably because he had plenty of time to think about them. For the most part, he kept to himself. He says, "I was never really good at sports . . . so I just made music." Gradually, Atkins turned from traditional instruments to electronic music. Perhaps inspired by the early high school social club parties,

Atkins picked up the DJ bug and started the DJ collective Deep Space, which would follow him well beyond graduation.

Technofy Your Mind

While hopscotching between Detroit and Belleville on the weekends, Atkins still found time to attend Washtenaw County Community College. It was there, in one of his music classes, that he met Richard ("Rik") Davis, a Vietnam War veteran and aspiring electronic musician. According to Atkins, Davis's material was "real abstract . . . avant-garde, electronic montage stuff." The two didn't do much in the way of socializing until Atkins handed Davis one of his early synth demo tapes. "Rik didn't want people to come by his place," says Atkins. "This was still during a time when you thought you had to get three or four people together to record. People were still in the mind-set of 'Hey, let's get everybody together and jam.'" But eventually and perhaps unexpectedly, Atkins was invited to check out Davis's studio. "Rik is a very isolated person," says Atkins. "There's still things that I don't know about him. He's just one of those people that are real secretive about certain things in his life."

In addition to a love for electronic music, Davis was well versed in the futurist theories of the day (as well as in biblical prophecy and various forms of mysticism). Somewhere in his reading and studies, Davis had decided on the pseudonym "3070," the significance of which he is not ready to reveal. "The purpose was simple," says Davis of his intent. "It was how to survive when the vultures and thieves came to take away what I had inserted into the cultural matrix!" It seemed Davis was taking a conceptual cue from Kraftwerk, who also reveled in the mnemonic and resonant qualities of numbers. In choosing the timeless symbolism of numbers, and perhaps even foreseeing the digital future, Davis was hoping to ensure that his contribution to techno would outlast changes in language and culture.

As Atkins and Davis began creating synthesized music in the studio, they also tinkered with language and created a dictionary that reflected their own predictions for the future, which they called "the grid." Essentially, the grid was just a growing list of recombinant compound words, but Atkins and Davis seemed to treat it more as their own Bible, the one source from which all of their new concepts would come. At the very least, one of their first entries would help get them noticed: "cybotron," which was fashioned from "cyborg" and "cyclotron," became the name under which they would record.

Musically, Cybotron was a complicated read. Though its similarities to Kraftwerk are too obvious to ignore, Atkins and Davis produced a sound that was more complicated, murky, and grim. The two groups also had very different vocalists: instead of the sharp vocal delivery of Kraftwerk's Ralf Hütter, Cybotron often featured Atkins's deep, resonant voice. Atkins suggests that, at least prior to meeting Davis, he was unaware of the German group.

> Yes, Kraftwerk was definitely an influence on my professional recording career. But this was two years after I had already been dealing with synthesizers. The beauty of first hearing Kraftwerk was that the sounds were so similar to what I was doing, and these guys were halfway across the planet. I knew it was electronic as soon as I heard it. But the thing is that their stuff was clean and precise . . . [while] I had all kinds of weird UFO sounds . . . it [Atkins's music] was [more] psychedelic.

The psychedelia in Atkins's music came through his love of George Clinton's Parliament-Funkadelic, which he had seen perform a number of times while growing up. In fact, Aaron Atkins believes that his brother picked up his guitar less and less after he heard what Parliament-Funkadelic member Bernie Worrell could do with keyboards.

Cybotron's first single, "Alleys of Your Mind," was released in 1981, apparently just after the landmark "Sharevari." Though it wasn't the first "techno" record to come out of Detroit, it became a much bigger success, proving that Cybotron's economy of language had more staying power than A Number of Names. Whereas "Sharevari" was a more direct extension of the music popular in the northwest side, "Alleys" reconnected those influences with the bedrock of funk that will always be a part of Detroit. Moreover, Cybotron helped make funk palatable and relevant again, rescuing it from the grandiosity of eleven-, twelve-, and twenty-piece bands, fright wigs, giant diapers, and elaborate stage sets—all with a little ditty about paranoia and thought control, recorded on a four-track tape machine.

The unusual subject matter and unique sound of "Alleys of Your Mind" caught the interest of a popular local DJ known as "the Electrifying Mojo." With Mojo's endorsement and support, Cybotron quickly grew into a local

Detroit phenomenon, selling copies directly to the plethora of local mom-and-pop record stores that still exist on both sides of the city. "Alleys of Your Mind" and its follow-up, "Cosmic Cars," got a lot of local radio play, as well as unit sales in the tens of thousands. Larger entities soon took notice.

"[Our second record was] being distributed by a local distributor [AMI]," Atkins remembers. "We were selling so many records that Bob Schwartz [the distributor] called up the independent distributor for Fantasy [Records]." This was a rather strange way to go about getting a record deal, especially since Cybotron certainly wasn't waiting for any A&R scouts to come knocking. Instead, Atkins had transformed Deep Space, his former DJ collective, into a label and publishing company for the group's records. "We weren't 'discovered,'" says Atkins. "We sold our own records on Deep Space—10,000 copies of 'Alleys of Your Mind' and 10,000–15,000 of 'Cosmic Cars'—before Fantasy even realized who we were. We didn't know anything about [Fantasy's interest] until one day we opened the mailbox and found a contract."

Cybotron's deal was even stranger considering its distance, both musically and geographically, from Fantasy. Based in Berkeley, California, Fantasy traces its roots to 1949 and early recordings by Dave Brubeck. Now part of the Concord Music Group, Fantasy continues to reissue a host of bebop, R&B, and classic jazz records. In the current Fantasy roster one can find Cybotron wedged between Creedence Clearwater Revival and the piano-driven rock of the Gabe Dixon Band.

In the 1980s, however, Fantasy had a commitment to more contemporary R&B and soul acts (including Pleasure, Sylvester, and Isaac Hayes), and saw potential in Cybotron's tangential funk. At the very least, Cybotron's success in Detroit proved that it could sell records. Despite the seeming lack of effort Fantasy put into promoting the group (not even so much as a publicity photo existed of it, outside of one Atkins and Davis had taken themselves at a local studio), Cybotron turned out to be a good gamble.

Fantasy's interest in Cybotron coincided with the birth of a sound known as "electro," presumably a shortening of "electronic funk." Electro was one of the great dance music developments of the early 1980s that was neither a derivation nor an extension of disco. Instead, it was a "switched-on" funk variant, exaggerating the electronic sounds that Midwestern groups like Parliament-Funkadelic had perfected in the studio and brought onstage. Most critics point to New York, however, for the genre's watershed moment.

Afrika Bambaataa and the Soulsonic Force—a group based in New York and backed by the great band Planet Patrol and producer Arthur Baker—took their love of Kraftwerk to extremes with "Planet Rock," a song that became the ultimate electro anthem. Recorded in 1982, "Planet Rock" was built on the melody of Kraftwerk's "Trans-Europe Express" and had a drum pattern similar to that in "Numbers," another Kraftwerk classic. Though Atkins and Davis had the Bambaataa crew beat by a year with "Alleys of Your Mind," they were still operating on a smaller scale and carried a much less jovial atmosphere: compare the opening of "Planet Rock," when Bambaataa beckons all the "party PEE-PLE" to the dance floor, with Cybotron's introverted walk through the "Alleys of Your Mind." Atkins remembers the immediate impact of "Planet Rock" well as he was in New York at the time, trying to promote Cybotron: "I was actually in New York with two or three boxes of 'Cosmic Cars'—taking them around, dropping them with different people that I knew, trying to see if I could get something going. Of course, you can't just walk into New York with some records—that's not how it works. The day I was leaving, 'Planet Rock' came on the air, and the [radio] station was like, 'We got it first, nyah, nyah!'"

The success of "Planet Rock" established Baker, Bambaataa, and company as early leaders of the electro genre, which became defined by their output and that of others from the New York area. Brooklyn groups Newcleus and Mantronix, the latter formed by Jamaican Kurtis Mantronik (Kurtis Khaleel), highlighted the mid-1980s East Coast scene. Groups on the West Coast were fewer but included standout talent Egyptian Lover (Greg Broussard), who paved the way for the huge West Coast hip-hop scene to come. (Rapper Ice-T even got his start on the old 1984 electro single "Reckless.") Notably absent amid all of this activity were records from the Midwest.

That all changed when Cybotron's debut album, *Enter*,[1] hit the streets in 1983. Looking back, it's hard to imagine an album with vocals, guitar riffs, and unambiguous swipes at the military-industrial complex—as much a progressive rock album as anything else—becoming a blueprint for today's electro and techno records. Yet hints of the instrumentation and song structures to come can be heard, buried in the genetic code of Detroit techno—the slight difference that set the genre apart from the neighboring Chicago house sound. Over two decades later, *Enter* is still sought after although, according to Atkins, it sold better as the CD reissue *Clear* than it ever did on the original vinyl pressing.

Especially when examined through the songs and themes of *Enter*, Cybotron seemed more like a band than any of techno's subsequent producers would ever be, even adding guitarist Jon Housley (aka Jon-5) to the lineup by the time the album was completed. Still, Cybotron was consciously trying to break the mold of rock 'n' roll groups and the process by which they get discovered. As Davis told the *Ann Arbor News* in 1983: "The days of immediate gratification are over. . . . There are just no more millionaire Colonel Tom Parkers walking around looking for the new Elvis Presley. Consequently, when we formed Cybotron, we decided that we'd always operate independently of the bar scene, and try to perfect our craft as recording artists. And to this day, we've never played in any bar or nightclub."[2]

Adding to the impact of *Enter*, the single "Clear" made a huge splash and became Cybotron's biggest hit, especially after it was remixed by Jose "Animal" Diaz. "Clear" climbed the charts in Dallas, Houston, and Miami, and spent nine weeks on the *Billboard* Top Black Singles chart (as it was called then) in fall 1983, peaking at No. 52. "Clear" was a success. And contrary to what soul music purists had claimed, "Clear" proved that electronic music *could* have soul. In other words, Atkins and Davis drew a new line in the definition of electronic music styles, representing a milestone in the fusion of electronic experimentation with funky dance music.

At the peak of Cybotron's success in 1983 and 1984, a difference in direction caused Atkins to set out on his own. Davis wanted to take the group's sound in a more rock-based direction and, what's more, the difference between "Clear" and its follow-up, "Techno City," was too great for Atkins: "I was against that record ['Techno City']. It's a great record, but it wasn't the right one to follow 'Clear.' I mean, we had black radio programmers eating out of our hands!" With the national impact of "Clear," techno might have developed quite differently had Cybotron stayed in the game.

It was during this period that freeform radio started to wane and MTV became an increasingly powerful force in cultural programming, leaving little room for an underground phenomenon like techno music. This was especially the case as hip-hop became *the* new music, obscuring nearly every other innovative sound. No one could have predicted the success of records like Run-DMC's "It's Like That" in 1983 or the Beastie Boys' smash

DETROIT, 1996: JUAN ATKINS AND "MAD" MIKE BANKS IN THE FIRST LIVE
PERFORMANCE OF MODEL 500. (Ian Malbon)

album *Licensed to Ill* in 1986. Undetected by listeners and critics alike, techno continued a more gradual evolution below the surface: few Cybotron fans traced the group back to Detroit after its split, or to the music that followed.

In 1985, a year after the release of "Techno City" and his departure from the group, Atkins took a track supposedly planned for Cybotron—"No UFOs"—and used it to launch Metroplex Records. Taking a numerical pseudonym of his own—Model 500—he embarked on a solo recording career. "I just put [DJing] to the side for a while," he says. "When I started Metroplex, the party scene had died down and there weren't any more lawn parties, social clubs, and things like that . . . and this was way before the international DJ scene."

Atkins's dedication to his new record label and a series of electro tracks, such as "Night Drive (Thru Babylon)" and "Technicolor,"[3] gave way to more straight four-count disco beats as early house sounds began to find their way into Detroit. "Play It Cool" was Metroplex's first experiment with the four-count beat structure, but it made Atkins's vocals sound out of place and lacking detached coolness of his first few records. Not until 1987 would Metroplex have its first proper "techno" success, with "Goodbye Kiss" by Eddie Fowlkes.

Atkins would eventually become techno's spiritual leader of sorts; some even called him "Obi Juan." This may stem in part from his laid-back personality—Atkins seems always on an even keel, and whatever frustrations he experiences in the act of creating music or dealing with the industry are simply not reflected in his outward appearance. The nickname is also, of course, a reflection of Atkins's contribution to the genre. Whether with Cybotron or his own Model 500 project, his work would continue to help keep techno conceptually complex. Of the sentiments behind the classic "No UFOs," for example, Atkins says: "The government always tells people what to think about, and seems to cover up the existence of UFOs. ['No UFOs' is] about thought control—taking away people's hope so that they don't look towards the future." Even more sinister sounding is "Night Drive (Thru Babylon)," which outlines a brilliant vignette of electro escapism via a jittery keyboard line and Atkins's whispered description of the ultimate Detroit trip.[4]

Freestyle

If Atkins was the prophet, the one to tap into the unseen and unheard possibilities of electronic music, Derrick May was the high priest who brought them about with forceful incantations. Born on June 4, 1963, in Detroit, May moved with his family to Belleville in the late 1970s. There, he became friends with Atkins, and with him started Deep Space. After his junior year of high school, May headed back to Detroit. "I was floatin'," says May. "My mom had moved to Chicago shortly after I moved down here [Detroit] and I was still in . . . my last year [of] high school. The year after I graduated, instead of going on to college to run track and play football, I just sort of floated and walked the streets. Sometimes I lived with [Atkins] and his grandmother. . . . The Atkins family was very good to me."

May took a markedly different route to becoming a DJ and musician than had his friend Atkins. While still spinning with Deep Space, he often went to visit his mother in Chicago, getting exposure to the city's sound through the radio on WBMX. May describes how Chicago radio influenced him.

> When I first heard the guys on the radio, I was surprised. I thought we were the only ones thinking and feeling this kind of music. . . . [Then] I heard some

new stuff alongside stuff that I [already] knew. I was thinking of moving there [to Chicago] just so I could hear [DJ] Farley Jack Master Funk and these guys playing Trax [a record label].

I also met some people and they took me to the Power Plant [where] I heard Frankie Knuckles play. Frankie was really a turning point in my life. . . . When I heard him play, and I saw the way people reacted, danced, and sang to the song—and fall in love with each other [to the music]—I *knew* this was something special. Not just being a DJ and playing music and being on a mission, but playing music with love. This vision of making a moment this euphoric . . . it changed me.

If May was somehow spiritually transformed by his experiences in Chicago, he was not at all blind to the professionalism of the Chicago scene. "I wanted to concentrate my elements on finding out how they did what they did and how to [take it] to the next level," he says. May's combination of Detroit and Chicago styles was first acknowledged when a radio music director heard about his work at a Detroit club. "There was this friend of a friend who was a music director there [at WJLB]," says May. "She had heard about me [spinning] at the Liedernacht, the first club where you had black kids and white kids dancing together to early house and Detroit records. This was back in 1985." May was offered a radio show called *Street Beat,* which usually preceded the Electrifying Mojo's show on WJLB.

In late 1986, May, sparking with determination and inspiration, followed Atkins to become the second Deep Space jock to set out on his own. His new label, Transmat, named after one of Atkins's techno-speak dictionary terms, was quickly set in motion. "I got 'Transmat' from his [Atkins's] song, 'Night Drive,'"[5] says May. "I didn't really care so much for what the concept of it was—I just liked the way it sounded." Originally intended to be a subsidiary of Atkins's Metroplex label, Transmat used the prefix MS (Metroplex Subsidiary) for cataloging purposes. The MS prefix was retained even after Transmat became its own entity, and is still used today. "I kept it [this prefix] as a tribute to Metroplex and all they did for me," he says. "Juan [Atkins] has been the most integral part of this whole thing; without him it really doesn't happen."

Having approached techno from less of a musician's perspective than had Atkins, May was the one to unearth its most surprising sounds and compositions. Not that this was apparent with Transmat's first twelve-inch single, "Let's Go." "When I made my first record, it was with Juan [Atkins]. I didn't like it, but then, I didn't do it. Having someone produce you when you think you know what you're doing, but you really don't, is really demoralizing. But I went along with it and I did the parts—the bassline and what have you—and Juan took the song and created it." In retrospect, "Let's Go" seems like a truly silly song—a kind of attempt at hip-hop with the same instruments May and Atkins were using to make techno. To boot, Atkins's brother Aaron gave the "lyrics" a loopy delivery.[6]

May's next song, however, would come to define techno more than any borrowed term from Alvin Toffler ever could. "Nude Photo," released in 1987 under May's new Rhythim Is Rhythim moniker, represented a totally different approach from that taken by Chicago house—closer to the vest and definitely more personal. It was also the first time May had used the Yamaha DX-100 keyboard.

Essentially a scaled-down, portable version of the larger DX-21 keyboard, the DX-100 has keys that were smaller and closer together. Its FM (frequency modulation) synthesis also offered an especially interesting bank of "analog" bass guitar sounds, which May would always play in the most inverted, staccato manner possible. "Nude Photo" helped define May's style, assimilating Atkins's purposefully electronic sounds with the more dynamic approach of Chicago house.

"Nude Photo" is also notable for a small bit of recurring controversy. Even though original pressings of the song list collaborator Tom Barnett as a writer, Barnett's contribution is frequently debated by fans and critics alike. Says May, "Tom Barnett originally had an idea for the song; he even had a concept for it. I listened to it and overnight I re-created the whole song. I didn't . . . use his version of the song, but because he had originally conceived the idea, he was part of it! And that's that."

May's most famous work, however, is his 1987 record "Strings of Life," built around his friend Michael James's piano licks and sampled strings from the Detroit Symphony Orchestra. Although May has many other compositions that are more challenging and even daring for their time—the more minimal "Kaos" with its out-of-control flange[7] effect, for example—"Strings" has held onto its popular status among DJs and casual listeners. To its credit, the song is still among techno's most dramatic.

While Atkins had played instruments since he was eleven years old, May was more of an alchemist, unearthing majestic sounds from his equipment. May went on to add new dimensions and colors with releases like "Beyond the Dance" and "The Beginning," taking techno in dozens of new directions at once and having, on a smaller scale, the kind of expansive impact John Coltrane had on jazz.

Pennies from Heaven

The youngest of Belleville's three emerging techno producers (they're each separated by a year), Kevin Saunderson was born in Brooklyn, New York, on May 9, 1964. When he was fifteen, his family moved to Belleville, where he eventually became high school friends with Atkins and May, even if at first he didn't share in their extensive music discussions. As May recalls, their bonding process was much less sophisticated: "Kevin and I were on the [Belleville High School] football team together, but we weren't friends right away. I used to make fun of him all the time, and one day I made fun of him too much and he actually punched me. [May laughs.] Well, we didn't get into a fight—he just knocked me out. After that we became the best of friends. I have a scar on my lip to this day." After high school, both Saunderson and Atkins stayed close to Belleville —Saunderson at Eastern Michigan University (EMU) and Atkins at Washtenaw Community College—and Saunderson joined Atkins's and May's Deep Space DJ collective.[8]

Although Saunderson would be the last of the Belleville transplants to take to techno music, he would also become the most successful, in very short order. Not that he wasn't busy enough at EMU—in addition to his studies, Saunderson had pledged Phi Beta Sigma fraternity and was still playing football. But the little exposure he got to the burgeoning techno scene would soon take over. Before long, his music hobby had outgrown the basement studio he had off-campus, and he eventually joined May's *Street Beat* radio show on WJLB. Saunderson remembers his entrance into the techno scene.

> Before Derrick's [May's] show, I was playing football for Eastern Michigan. I eventually decided that was it: I wasn't going to make it to the pros at that school, so I took another angle and started [DJing]. After I saw Eddie Fowlkes spin at a fraternity party, I jumped into the clique [Deep Space] and started practicing my ass off. *Street Beat* was different because it wasn't just mixing, but edits, using the pause button, creating wild sounds, and all that. You'd basically do a whole

KEVIN SAUNDERSON AND DERRICK MAY, ALSO KNOWN
AS THE "ELEVATOR" AND THE "INNOVATOR."
(Doug Coombe)

new production . . . getting creative with someone else's record. I took that
concept from Derrick.

It was in May's basement studio that Saunderson wrote his way out of
school and into the music industry. In 1985 he started KMS records, an
acronym for Kevin Maurice Saunderson.[9] In addition to writing some of
the most brutal Detroit techno of the late 1980s with his friend and school-
mate Santonio Echols,[10] Saunderson also dabbled in more "above-ground"
pursuits, namely pop-oriented dance music with vocals. "I was really surprised when he wanted to do 'Triangle of Love,'" recalls Detroit DJ Art

Payne. "Everyone else was making these little sample tracks, but he saw that he wanted to go beyond that and . . . make a 'real' record, more or less. He was always the one who had a vision and then did whatever he could to get to where he wanted to be."

Saunderson's next experiment with vocals would become as important, and controversial, as May's "Nude Photo." Still tinkering in his basement studio, Saunderson enlisted the help of James "Jit" Pennington and Art Forrest, who respectively came up with the rhythm and melody for "Big Fun," an upbeat pop/house crossover tune. Pennington, Forrest, and Roy Holmon (who cowrote the follow-up single "Good Life") were apparently paid musician's scale for their work, which was fine in the meantime—"Big Fun" hadn't become a huge hit just yet.

Saunderson, Pennington, and Holmon soon formed a group called Inner City, recording (and even performing) "Big Fun" with another vocalist. But on the recommendation of Chicago producer Terry "Housemaster" Baldwin, Saunderson switched to the talents of Paris Grey, who was already established as a house music vocalist. Grey, born Shanna Jackson on November 5, 1965, came from a large family in the Chicago area and had been singing since she was five years old. With Grey's vocals and lyrics, "Big Fun" was destined for radio play and success. *Big Fun,* the album, was released in 1989 and spawned a total of four singles ("Big Fun," "Good Life," "Ain't Nobody Better," and "Do You Love What You Feel"), all of which reached No. 1 on *Billboard*'s Hot Dance Music chart in 1989. "Big Fun" also cracked the *Billboard* Hot R&B Singles chart, and "Good Life" made the *Billboard* Hot 100 Singles chart.

When it came time to take Inner City on the road, Saunderson replaced Pennington and Holmon with Dennis White, a member of the Detroit alternative band Charm Farm, and Tommy Onyx (who cowrote a few songs on the band's second album, *Fire*). The band was complete when Darrell "D" Wynn was added as Inner City's DJ.

Hitting the U.K. Top 40 eight times and selling close to six million records, Inner City would go on to become one of techno's greatest market successes of the 1980s, largely due to the talents and vision of Kevin Saunderson. "Kevin had a knack for pulling the right people together to get the job done," says Payne, by this time working promotions for KMS. "He was real good at that."

Techno Boulevard

As these early techno artists emerged, collaboration, determination, and synergy began flowing from their studios, slowly building to create a local scene. Metroplex, Transmat, and KMS all set up shop in the same building on Gratiot Avenue—soon to be called "Techno Boulevard"—in Detroit's Eastern Market. There's nothing particularly inspiring about Eastern Market, unless you happen to be up and among the haggling crowds buying fruits and vegetables on Saturday mornings, generally experiencing a pocket of the city that still "works," much the way it has for decades. Perhaps it was this modest spirit that attracted techno's early producers. There, the close proximity of their studios allowed them to learn from one another and to fine-tune their skills by remixing each other's material.

As this techno scene developed, a semiformal progression emerged by which DJs would become promoted to full-fledged artists and producers. Digital recording techniques were not yet commonplace, so most recordings were put on reel-to-reel tape. Then came the time-consuming job of editing tape (a real chore before things went digital), a task that young, aspiring DJs were only too happy to perform as it meant becoming a part of the process—and sometimes even getting small credits on a label. As in spinning, tape editing requires a good ear for continuity and extreme patience. One signature trick used in Detroit techno is simply editing in a reversed segment or "bar" of music, mimicking DJ backspins and "rewinds." From the editing stage, some DJs plunged right into buying their own equipment; others took smaller steps, moving from editing to remixing to drum programming.

This progression functioned almost like a caste system until technology became more sophisticated and cheaper. In other words, it didn't last long, but long enough to bring some new talent into Detroit's collective. "I was a DJ, and I had a friend who taught me how to do tape edits, but I didn't come from that perspective," says Anthony Shakir, later a Detroit techno producer. "I was just mixing; I didn't know that they [mixing and editing] were intertwined. My thing was trying to learn how to make music and the only reason I got into electronic music was . . . that the early 1980s R&B just sucked. [I didn't like] the last Parliament Record, *Trombipulation,* so I started finding out about these other records." Shakir, or "Shake" as

A STRETCH OF GRATIOT NEAR EASTERN MARKET, A.K.A. "TECHNO BOULEVARD."
(Hans Veneman)

he's usually known, was one of many musicians, DJs, promoters, and A&R personnel to converge on Techno Boulevard, filling some of the roles necessary to keep the three main labels running while their owners were out performing.

Connection Machines

Before it found a geographical locus on Techno Boulevard, techno's development was easier to trace on the airwaves. As in a lot of other cities, the radio served as a great equalizer, bringing music that was formerly the province of select crowds (such as the preps, jits, or the gay community) to wider acceptance. In Chicago, for example, WBMX is often listed as a chief influence and breeding ground for the house music sound. Farley "Jackmaster" Funk (aka Farley Keith) was the first to land a spot on WBMX, where he pioneered house music mix shows that featured such talented DJs as Mario Diaz, Steve "Silk" Hurley, Mickey Oliver, Julian Perez, and Ralphie Rosario. Many of these DJs would go on to become producers as well.

In Detroit, radio has spawned fewer nationally recognized recording artists, but it has been home to many influential DJs, including Dwayne

"In the Mix" Bradley, who was best known for his "midday cuisine mix" on Detroit's WJLB. There were, however, two enigmatic DJs who commanded the city's airwaves like no others and led the city through the cross-pollination and transitional stages of the 1980s.

Charles Johnson grew up in Little Rock and Stuttgart, Arkansas, listening to a variety of blues, gospel, and rock sounds mixed together on the radio stations of the south. His own radio debut came in the Philippines (presumably part of a stint in some branch of the service), and to this day you can catch him rattling off an occasional greeting in Tagalog. After a few jobs back in Little Rock, he settled into a slot at WAAM, an AM rock station in Ann Arbor, Michigan. It was there that Johnson became "the Electrifying Mojo" (or simply "Mojo"), a change coinciding with a deeper personal transformation. As Johnson recalls:

> Back in 1972 I started to become suspicious of all [the] things I'd learned from radio, of what I'd been taught . . . all of the traditional approaches. I decided to lock myself away for about two weeks . . . to fast . . . to purge myself of all of the inept and non-applicable knowledge that I had attained, and to think my own thoughts based on things that were applicable to my own life. Everyone and everything got a fresh start and a fresh new assessment from my own personal reexamination.

Johnson's new outlook on life was most evident in his changed approach to procuring and presenting the content of his radio show. "I started going to the production room," he says. "I got real curious as to why they made records that [seemed] destined to become production fodder. Were they legitimately placed in that category? Or were they placed there by some of the same people that were programmed like I had been programmed?" Some of this so-called production fodder turned out to be the early electronic atmospherics of Tangerine Dream and Kraftwerk, whose music apparently served no better purpose at the time than backing tracks for commercials and promotions. "I remember when 'Trans-Europe Express' came out," remembers Johnson. "I played it and they [the station executives] said, 'What the hell is he playing now?' It wasn't a beat that people understood, but I could hear it perfectly. I mean, here's a band who's obviously from the same planet that I'm from, right?"

Johnson's weird mix of European instrumentals, new wave, funk, rock, soul, and anything else that fit the mood (he used to call his approach "mood-mats" as opposed to "formats") defied all predictions of radio executives and delighted audiences. By the time he began his grand tour of the Detroit radio dial,[11] Johnson knew that his mission would be connecting like-minded souls over the FM band. "From my perspective, radio was not going to be an instrument of divisiveness," says Johnson. "I would go and bridge the gap that separated young from old, rich from poor, black from white, and informed from uninformed, as opposed to my joining the circle of radio celebs who pretty much dominated the airwaves and psyche of people."

Johnson is still careful not to let his image or specific dates in his background leak out and detract from his music and message. He has managed an entire career without ever being photographed (even in his promotional head shot he appears in shadow), and in the process has created a radio "non-persona" that will last forever in the minds of Detroit radio audiences. Johnson's image was also fostered through elaborate theatrics used to fill out his late-night shows. Usually beginning with classical music, sci-fi soundtracks, or equally dramatic themes, Johnson would "arrive" in his mother ship each night—a process that often ate up the better part of half an hour. He would then segue into his nightly words of wisdom, which invariably ended with the following: "Whenever you feel that you're nearing the end of your rope, just tie a knot and keep hangin'." Johnson was everything Detroit needed at the time: something upbeat, mysterious, and eclectic.

Johnson was instrumental in making the traditionally "black" sounds of Parliament-Funkadelic, the Gap Band, and Cameo popular among white audiences, and in helping "white" groups like the B-52's and the J. Geils Band (both of which have paid Johnson on-air "thank you" visits) create a black fan base when they hadn't necessarily counted on one. And, in an era when mix-ups like these were still possible, Johnson may have had a hand in creating one of the time's largest crossover acts, single-handedly bringing Prince's music to Detroit and establishing one of his largest and most loyal followings.[12]

Though he eventually caved when Run-DMC rose to popularity, one thing Johnson didn't fully embrace was hip-hop. To this day, Johnson is highly critical of some of the paths down which hip-hop has progressed, specifically gangsta-rap. On the gate-fold of his self-published 539-page opus, *The Mental Machine,* Johnson takes the music industry to task, posting a warning "to all record companies who continue to manufacture the insidious soundtrack to genocide."[13]

If Johnson was tentative in accepting hip-hop, "the Wizard" reveled in it. "The Wizard" was the first guise of current techno demigod Jeff Mills, adopted back when he was merely an infamous, no-holds-barred technical DJ. Born in Detroit on June 18, 1963, Mills hailed from the northwest side, though he attended Mackenzie High School further to the south. Despite his interest in music and innate DJ talent, Mills managed not to become heavily involved with the high school party scene (though that era probably left a stylistic imprint: he can sometimes be found performing in button-down shirts, slacks, and even jackets). He *did* learn from the jocks of that era, however, through his older brother's association with the Dale Willis Organization, which featured Willis, Charles Hicks, Felton Howard, Ken Collier, and Stacey Hale, just to name a few. Though Mills started DJing in 1979 and 1980—his last two years in high school— his musical career didn't take top priority until he had spent a few years studying architecture.

Jeff Mills amazed crowds all over southeastern Michigan with his DJ skills—from Cheeks, a nightclub on Eight Mile Road in Detroit, to the Nectarine Ballroom in downtown Ann Arbor. John Collins, the resident DJ at Cheeks, hired Mills as an additional jock for the club. "When he auditioned, we were totally blown away by his skills and how fast he was with his hands," says Collins. "No one had ever really done what he was doing. I couldn't believe my eyes and ears."

Mills also figured prominently on the radio, eventually becoming as popular as Johnson, who had given him a guest spot on his show early on. Based on his growing fan base, Mills was given his own extensive mix show on Detroit's WDRQ. On his show, Mills became the Wizard—and never spoke a word. Presumably, speaking would have been a waste of airtime; instead, he used the time to cue up more records. Mills went on to perfect his eccentric hip-hop style of spinning and mixing and applied it to early electro, new wave, and house music. Like Johnson, almost nothing was off limits.[14]

Besides being more open than Mojo to the latest hip-hop sounds, Mills also pushed the boundaries of what could be done in the context of both radio mix shows and live DJ sets. At least as early as the 1980s, mix shows had almost always been created beforehand by street DJs like Mills. These

DJs recorded on portable four-track recorders that allowed several different inputs to be blended into a dense thicket of beats, vocals, and anything else that added complexity and intensity. Another four-track trick was to record at a slower pitch so that the on-air playback would be significantly faster. Amazingly, many aspiring jocks (including Mills himself) figured out ways to accomplish this in real time. With only two turntables and a stack of records, they would cue up the records and then tear through them with blazing speed—a modern equivalent of sorts to plate-spinning jugglers. Mills remembers it the other way around, starting with a very early exposure and access to three turntables.

> I used to have three turntables at WDRQ. The spare one was given in case there was a mechanical error while on the air. I eventually began to use it to create a more complex impression. The station gave me a Otari 2-track tape player and recorder. With this, I was shown how to edit tape to create master mixes for WDRQ and sister stations in other cities. With it, I began to create special versions of songs and would mix these remixes during the show. Multitracks (4-track recorders) weren't used until I moved to WJLB. By then, I had built a home studio where I could spend even more time creating content for each Wizard Show.

The amount of programming freedom that was handed to Jeff Mills was matched only by the Electrifying Mojo. In fact, their rivalry allowed Mills more and more access to equipment and production tools. The radio stations were that serious about their late-night jocks. Says Mills, "It was apparent that everyone had something to prove." WDRQ brought Jim Snowden in from New York's WBLS where he worked with Frankie "Hollywood" Crocker and hip-hop legends such as Marley Marl and Red Alert. Snowden hired Mills to bring a similar level of savvy to the station.

> When [Snowden] came to Detroit and WDRQ, he wanted very much to create a situation like NY Radio and was on the hunt to find a DJ from street. It was my position to compete with Mojo, so to give me complete and full freedom to play whatever was essential. To enhance this, I was given full access the record library WDRQ had and also a budget to purchase music. Later, I requested the authority to use the production studio and massive sound effects library. So, I could basically do anything and at almost anytime. There was a time that I could just abruptly interrupt normal programming and mix a few records just to keep

people on the edge. It was really fantastic. From these freedoms Mojo and I had, it created a lot of excitement because it gave impressions that radio was organic and free-flowing.

Mills's mastery of multiple genres,[15] thematic approaches, and technical precision have helped him rise to the very top of the DJ profession. Today, he is a respected techno artist and composer, yet still very much in demand as a DJ. Claude Young, who came up through the ranks much later and has recorded for Frictional, Seventh City Recordings, and the Belgian label Elypsia, has this to say of the man to whom he's often compared: "Anybody who says that Jeff Mills was not an influence during that time period [the 1980s] is lying. Jeff took the hip-hop attitude to dance music, and as far as I know, no one else has approached it that way."

Signal to Noise

The work of Mills and Johnson helped give the techno scene solid beginnings in Detroit. And while adventurous radio programmers would become harder and harder to find as the 1980s rolled on, there were still a few other savvy media entities that "got" techno, recognizing the distinct Detroit sound and its potential. Radio shows like *Fast Forward,* for example, became essential to techno's support network, helping galvanize interest and plant the seeds of a local scene that had a whole lot of growing to do.

Alan Oldham (later techno artist DJ T-1000) hosted *Fast Forward* from 1987 to 1992, making the most of late-night time slots on Detroit public radio. Broadcasting from Wayne State University's WDET, a National Public Radio affiliate, Oldham exposed listeners to techno, industrial, and everything else, from hip-hop to punk to Deee-Lite's electronic pop music. This mix was at its most interesting in the very early 1990s, when each style was borrowing heavily from the others. *Fast Forward* also provided a window to the explosive impact techno was beginning to have in the United Kingdom, long before glossy British dance music magazines began finding their way into hip U.S. record stores and bookstore chains with acres of magazine racks.

Institutionalized

Just as Oldham's Friday night *Fast Forward* slot would draw to a close at 3:00 A.M., another pillar of Detroit's nightly techno scene of the late 1980s would be reaching the apex of its activity. The Music Institute (MI), a legendary club, was as much a grand achievement for the scene in Detroit as any chart position or future release on Virgin Records. Club "architects" George Baker and Alton Miller were largely responsible for solidifying Detroit's techno scene of the time, giving artists a place to exercise their DJ skills and play their records without jetting across the Atlantic to the United Kingdom (which was by then offering a wider market for techno).

Located in downtown Detroit, the MI opened in the summer of 1988 and became home to Miller, Darrell ("D") Wynn, and Chez Damier (Anthony Pearson)—the core of the DJ lineup each weekend. Miller and Damier would spin for the primarily gay crowds on Saturday nights, and Wynn would team up with Derrick May most Fridays. As May remembers:

> It was funny, because I had picked that building out about five years before George even saw it, and I said this would be the perfect building for a club. Then George went and *got* the building. . . . I couldn't believe it! From there it all came together . . . we all contributed. I played there for a year for nothing; I never got paid, not a dime, for one year. The institute was a tribute to all that we put our hearts and souls into. It was a blessing.

The MI seemed to bring back the days (and most of the clientele) of the preps and social cliques era of the early 1980s. For a short time, divisions of class and sexual preference vanished once again, letting Detroit's collective black bohemia express itself the way it wanted. Inside, the DJ booth was raised on a platform almost a full story above the dance floor, set against the dark background of the MI's high ceilings. On the floor, the sounds were overwhelming and kick drums resonated in your chest cavity. Lights were almost an afterthought, so the only thing to do was dance —until 6 A.M.

Unfortunately, Detroit was still not ready to support sophisticated nightclubs, and the MI was doomed to suffer the same fate as the earlier high school clubs, closing one year later in 1989. However, as May explains, the MI's brief life may have been a blessing:

> I think that it all happened at the right time by mistake, and it didn't last because it wasn't supposed to last. Our careers took off right around the time we [the MI] had to close, and maybe it was the best thing. I think we were peaking—we were

so full of energy and we didn't know who we were or [how to] realize our potential. We . . . had no inhibitions, no standards—we just did it. That's why it came off so fresh and so innovative, and that's why . . . we got the best of the best.

May helped bring the MI to a close on November 24, 1989, mixing the ringing of recorded clock tower bells with his classic "Strings of Life." It was a dramatic end to a very short era. And even now, after having spun in such faraway places as South Africa and Chile, May still can't help but be amazed at the achievement of the Music Institute.

It was unbelievable, because it [techno] was new . . . and people [had] never heard it before. We had people driving in from Atlanta . . . New York, Chicago, just to come to the parties. Entertainers would come down to see the club and what it was all about, because it was something special. And I think that's why it lives on [symbolically] today. A lot of clubs have been around longer and have had much more prosperous "careers" . . . but the Music Institute is one of those places that died young and famous. It's like the *Titanic*—it just lives.

The Music Institute will forever remain a mythical part of techno, due in part to its short-lived energy and brilliance and to the way it functioned as a "home" for the music, transforming one of the city's old structures and putting it to work for a change. At the very least, it gave the emerging music enough "pull" to attract big-name visitors like Depeche Mode and ABC (which May skillfully remixed on its "Greatest Love of All" single), and others like Matt Cogger, who came to the MI to learn and then went on to record as Neuropolitique. Along with Detroit's early techno pioneers, the Music Institute helped give life to one of the city's important musical subcultures—one that was slowly growing into an international phenomenon.

4

Nation to Nation

Finding a Home in
Britain's Rave Culture,
1988–1991

In order for techno to transcend the inherent obscurity of the American Midwest, it had to literally widen its horizons. Oddly enough, this would happen not in other regions of the United States but across the Atlantic in the United Kingdom. Even more surprisingly, it would happen in only three short years. Between 1988 and 1990, techno would become radically transformed.

British audiences had long been interested in American music, having followed its inventive and soulful sounds all the way back to the Motown and Chess labels of the 1960s and 1970s. By the late 1980s, Chicago's latest interpretation of soul—house music—had already caught on in London's clubs and record shops. Steve "Silk" Hurley's "Jack Your Body" was a hit, the catalogs of DJ International, Trax, and Dance Mania were being combed by British DJs, and house artist Frankie Knuckles had even been interviewed by the British music magazine *NME*.

What England hadn't counted on, however, was another wave of musicians from Detroit—perhaps the feeling was that Parliament-Funkadelic, which had released its last record in 1980, was the end of the line. The odd Detroit record did make it overseas—even Was (Not Was) had minor success with "Woodwork Squeaks" in 1981. But through the late 1980s, the United Kingdom's firmest reference (and reverence) for Detroit was through Motown—especially the smaller, more obscure labels that were owned and/or started by Motown's producers in their spare time, such as Ric-tic, Wingate, and Golden World. These labels were the focus and prized possessions of England's "Northern Soul" devotees. Northern Soul was the nickname for the higher-energy American soul records (think "I Can't Help Myself (Sugar Pie Honey Bunch)" by the Four Tops and go from there). These records were scooped up and danced to in frenetic fashion by fans originally concentrated in England's northern urban centers in just one of many parallels to the rave culture that would follow a few decades later.

New Forms

One of the first Brits to hear Detroit's "new" sound was a fanatical record collector and Northern Soul fan from Birmingham named Neil Rushton. As head of Kool Kat Records, Rushton had been on a record-buying excursion in Chicago, with the ulterior motive of signing some house music acts to his label. While there, he learned about the Detroit sound and altered his travel plans midstream, detouring through Detroit on his way back to England. "I first made contact with Derrick [May]," he recalls. "Derrick came over to England [and] told me about Kevin [Saunderson]. Because of that, I called Kevin and licensed 'Nude Photo,' 'The Sound,' 'Our Music,' and 'Groovin' without a Doubt.' I realized that there was a whole movement there, and we [needed to move quickly] to exploit it."

Nothing gets past the obsessive record-collector mentality, and Rushton was quick to make the connection between this new sound and Detroit's legacy of great soul music, even if techno's artists tended to downplay it. Taking his cue from Motown and its frequent use of compilation albums, Rushton decided to release a compilation of the Detroit sound. As Rushton explains: "We'd done an English house record, 'House Reaction,' at Virgin and I got to know Mick Clark . . . who's also an old soul fan. . . . He [Clark] was into this whole idea of Detroit. So I sold him on the idea of doing a compilation, which I suppose was subliminally connected to the old Motown compilations. You'd buy these compilations with twelve acts, like the Marvellettes and the Contours."

Rushton plunged into the project (which would actually be released on Virgin's now defunct "10" imprint), even getting right in the middle of some of Detroit's first battles—including a complicated sampling imbroglio involving Reese & Santonio's first record, "The Sound," which, according to Rushton, had been "ripped off" (liberally sampled) by Todd Terry, a pioneer of the New York house sound.

By 1988, Rushton was acting more like a manager than an A&R scout, which is exactly what he had become by the time the compilation project got underway. It all seemed a bit much for one person to sort out from across the Atlantic. Explains Rushton:

> Derrick [May] was my main port of call, but I licensed tracks from Derrick, Kevin [Saunderson], and Juan [Atkins]—Transmat, KMS, and Metroplex. . . . We were licensing stuff from people who didn't actually have the records. That became quite a mess later. Checks that were allegedly forged and all kinds of things between people in Detroit. We basically did a deal where there was a budget of £20,000 [roughly U.S. $31,500]. I [had] told everybody that . . . if it didn't recoup, there [wouldn't be any] money ever made. And it never recouped.

Back home in Detroit, Derrick May was doing some scrambling of his own, keeping the dialogue with Rushton going and essentially working as a production coordinator on the compilation. As May recalls, it was one of his busiest times.

> I was working with Carl [Craig], helping Kevin, helping Juan, trying to put Neil Rushton in the right position to meet everybody, trying get Blake [Detroit DJ and techno artist Blake Baxter] endorsed so that everyone liked him, trying to convince Shake [Detroit techno producer Anthony Shakir] that he should be more assertive . . . and keep making music as well as do the Mayday mix [for his *Street Beat* show on WJLB] and run Transmat records. . . . For years, no one [had] cared about what Juan and I were doing in Detroit, and then I found myself dealing with people that were jealous, out of the clear blue sky.

Despite these early rumblings of dissension, the Detroit techno scene was unified enough to push the new compilation forward. At this point, the album's tentative title was *The House Sound of Detroit,* with graphics similar to those on the compilations coming from Chicago—but fate had other plans.

One of the last artists to contribute to the compilation was Atkins, who had just returned from an extended trip to California. Atkins turned in a song called "Techno Music," which used the same integration of speech synthesis Kraftwerk had used throughout its 1981 album *Computer World.*[1] The voice "sang" out repeated refrains of "I program my home computer" and "techno music." Rushton was instantly prompted to change the compilation's title to *Techno! The New Dance Sound of Detroit.* Just like that, the name for Detroit's dance music was born, setting it apart from house and defining it as a new musical genre in its own right.

Ironically, the song that carried the compilation to its initial prominence was another late add-on—Inner City's "Big Fun." Nobody had planned on this experiment becoming the monster hit it did—not even Rushton, who picked it up for the album only after returning to Detroit to finalize the project. As Rushton recalls:

> However many tracks we were supposed to deliver to Virgin—ten or twelve— we were still missing one. I had stayed over in Detroit longer than I had planned, canceling my flight and all that, because I had to come back with the whole album. Derrick [May] even made a record while I was there ["It Is What It Is"], and because [the compilation] was short of a track, I stayed up all night while he did that. No one had any tracks—we ran out of ones that were good enough. On the very last day . . . Kevin came over to Derrick's with a whole load of tapes to sort it out, and he brought "Big Fun."

As it turned out, "Big Fun" would be a fortunate choice—it went on to become a Top 10 hit on the U.K. Gallup Top 40 in fall 1988, throwing Saunderson and partner Paris Grey into the wild world of pop stardom. Saunderson, who typifies the reserved and introspective techno producer to a degree, initially seemed uncomfortable with his newfound success. But then, Atkins, May, and Saunderson each had his own way of relating to the hype surrounding the compilation. "Kevin, Juan, and Derrick were such good people to interview in different ways," Rushton offers. "Kevin being really nice and playing the 'genial giant,' even though his music's dead powerful and represents the way he looks. Juan was so soft-spoken [and] inter-

A SAMPLE OF VIRGIN RECORDS' MARKETING EFFORTS FOR THE
FIRST TECHNO MUSIC COMPILATION IN 1988.

esting, and Derrick because he's completely mad. People loved Derrick. . . .
he was a complete star from the moment you met him."

Although perhaps more psychologically prepared than Atkins or
Saunderson, May was astounded by the transformation from unknown mu-
sical experimentation in Detroit to Virgin's summer 1988 kickoff party in
London.[2] Louise Gray of the English magazine *City Limits* caught up with
May right after his arrival in London. In her article "Paradise Revisited," she
described a fraction of the hype surrounding the compilation: "Having

spent the last eighteen hours in a studio producing [London's] Adrenalin MOD for MCA Records,[3] his room's littered with 'dear Derrick' letters; Boy George's on the phone; a mix of Kraftwerk, Ultravox, and Stevie Wonder's 'Life of Plants' is on the ghetto blaster; outside the A&R execs are queuing for the privilege of wining, dining, and signing the twenty-five-year-old—the human face of machine music."[4]

Techno's early success in London was hard to measure. Despite the hype and press coverage of the producers and DJs involved, the *Techno!* compilation did not sell as well as Virgin had hoped. The simple fact was that it didn't sit well with buyers or with the collective attention span of London—one of the harshest environments for new musical trends. Though Londoners had accepted techno in the form of club entertainment or isolated singles, perhaps they weren't yet ready for an entire double album of the music.

Not that London didn't have its share of early techno adopters and enthusiasts. Among them were writers like Stuart Cosgrove, whose article "Seventh City Techno" was one of the few bits of English press from that era to leak back into the United States. In his article for *The Face,* Cosgrove asserted that Detroit's sound "refutes the past" and described it as "post-soul"[5]—interesting demarcations that further separated techno from Chicago house. Though only partially accurate—techno has an obvious relationship to soul and even to Motown—he helped give the music a new code and mystique that helped grow its U.K. fan base.

In fact, once Rushton and Atkins set Detroit apart with the *Techno!* compilation, the music took off on its own course, no longer parallel to the Windy City's progeny. And as the 1980s came to a close, the difference between techno and house music became increasingly pronounced, with techno's instrumentation growing more and more adventurous. Unfortunately, as techno went on to progress and pick up influences across Europe in the early 1990s, this distinction would become a liability of sorts. American audiences and critics would start associating the term "techno" almost exclusively with harsh European components of the music, and even with the more academic side of electronic music, which has a neat European lineage and explanation. As Atkins explains:

> As far as I know, nobody had applied technology to music using that term ["techno"], especially in dance music. You had electronic musicians out there, but most of them were really abstract. Nobody's claiming that we invented elec-

tronic music. Some people tend to think of it that way and they get all bent out of shape. Techno is something that just happened. People looked at you like you have some big, preconceived plan, [but] it's the general public who designated us to be who we are.

In the wake of the *Techno!* compilation, things started to happen more organically for the Detroit artists. If nothing else, techno's introduction to London had given its artists the freedom to explore broader possibilities within the industry. There were, of course, the expected false starts and stunted opportunities. One was a brief chance for Saunderson and May to help produce an album for Herbie Hancock (who has often investigated the latest dance music trends), but Hancock simply lost interest before things got started.

A second opportunity was the idea to form a supergroup with May, Saunderson, and Atkins. The idea was quickly pared down to just May and Atkins, as Saunderson's success with Inner City left him no choice but to stick with the duo's trajectory. May and Atkins, who were going to be known as Intellex, were attempting to negotiate a deal with ZTT when things fell apart.[6] As Rushton, who was still May's and Atkins's manager at the time, recalls:

We started discussions with ZTT—who's been there since the early days, Art of Noise and all that. They . . . wanted to join in on techno and he had this really dreadful idea that they [May and Atkins] would be the black Pet Shop Boys. I said, "Oh shit, that's not what we want is it?" But Derrick said, "No, it'll be great!" We went through all these negotiations [and] got this contract done, a massive, non-exclusive deal . . . and it was a lot of money, really, for what it was.

Unfortunately, communication between May and Rushton got lost because of some other side issue, and the ZTT deal fell through. Rushton explains: "We got an anguished call from [ZTT] saying, 'We can't do it because Derrick won't go on *Top of the Pops.*' I said, 'Well, that's OK. That's part of the allure, isn't it? You can't have [an underground artist like] Derrick May on *Top of the Pops,* can you?' The whole thing collapsed and I got blamed for that. It was an ultimate contrast in expectations—a U.K. record company trying to be hip."

Despite the first *Techno!* compilation's lukewarm reception, there was enough interest and impetus for Virgin to release a follow-up compilation,

Techno 2: The Next Generation, in 1990. *Techno 2* introduced the new talents of the Detroit scene, such as Carl Craig, Octave One, and Jay Denham (aka Fade 2 Black). Unfortunately, fickle London audiences and the press seemed to have tired of techno for the time being and failed to appreciate the talent and more focused approach of the new compilation. Or, as Octave One's Lenny Burden puts it, "The fad was over. . . . The second album came out and the people were like, 'Okay, we've heard techno, we need something else.'"

Flashback

While commercial success and popular appeal temporarily eluded techno, a different type of dance music took London by storm. Acid house, another variant of the Chicago house sound, came into prominence as early as 1985, within only a year of its inception. Named for its psychedelic sounds, "acid" had developed in the mid-1980s when artists like the Chicago house outfit Phuture began experimenting with the Roland TB-303 synthesizer. The 303 was originally marketed as a bassline generator to accompany solo musicians—much the way drum machines were first used. It had a unique onboard sequencer, a resonance filter, and generally a rich or "fat" sound. The result, as Phuture's Spanky, Herbert J., and DJ Pierre found, was a syrupy squelch that had almost nothing in common with a bass guitar. Instead, the 303 emitted aural equivalents of liquid mercury—the sounds of psychedelic hallucination. The name "acid" was a natural fit.

Phuture's single "Acid Trax," released in 1987, featured the 303 in the forefront and Chicago's trademark bare-bones drum sound underneath. The song was soon popularized by DJ Ron Hardy—so much so that it became known as "Ron Hardy's Acid Track." Several copycats and permutations later, Chicago found itself giving birth to the acid house phenomenon.

By 1988 acid house was blowing London away—the drug connotations of the term "acid" were a perfect complement for the increasingly popular rave movement, providing the catalyst for a monumental cultural shift. Though in many ways they felt foreign to this process, Detroit's techno artists found themselves getting involved with the new music scene and collaborating with acid house DJs. As a result of these collaborations and their refined DJ skills, they became a bankable talent in the United Kingdom.

Within a year, Detroit DJs were getting booked in English clubs regularly, and weekend junkets turned into extended vacations and career explorations as they began to make friends with similar artists. One of these was the well-established Mark Moore, the producer behind the sample-pop-acid house sensation S'Express. Moore was also the center of a growing transatlantic clique that included English techno artist Peter "Baby" Ford, among others. "[We] were a small group of people that took it [techno and acid house] in quite a deep way," says Ford. "Techno was some kind of revolutionary musical form—that I still believe. It was crossing cultures, crossing the Atlantic and everything."

In 1988 both Ford and Moore were signed to the U.K. label Rhythm King, which quickly rose to prominence based on the ingenious songwriting abilities of its dance music artists. Together with Tim Simenon's Bomb the Bass project, Ford and Moore created some of the most subversive and energetic pop music ever recorded. Ford's first album, *Ford Trax,* wasn't so much an album as a collection of his finest dance tracks (as the title might suggest). "Flowers" and "Chikki Chikki Ahh Ahh" were incredibly dense, psychedelic, and positive singles—even more so than some of the first-generation Chicago acid house offerings. Ford's follow-up, *Ooo, the World of Baby Ford,* while perhaps not as successful as Moore's *Original Soundtrack,* showed that dance music *could* cross over, be successful, and still be inventive.

Unlike ZTT (according to Rushton's critical assessment of it), the Rhythm King label was hip enough to take a chance on untested talent. Case in point was Sarah Gregory, an English makeup artist, painter, and (eventually) singer. Gregory befriended May and protégé Carl Craig during this period of Rhythm King's heyday, in 1988–89. (Gregory even visited the Music Institute in Detroit, painting a mural on its largest wall.) Eventually, Gregory joined forces with Craig, adding her vocal to a whole series of tracks he had recorded on a small, humble setup on the carpeted floor of a West London flat. This collaboration had the potential to be a great crossover of Detroit and London dance music styles, with May and Ford also lending a hand. Sadly, the project never materialized.[7] As Ford explains:

> They [Rhythm King] all lost their interest in dance music right about 1992 [and] went into a pop/rock label. It's all very sad really. Rhythm King started with a

. . . really inspired . . . team of people—mainly artists and DJs to start with [such as] Colin Faver, Eddie Richards, Mark Moore, Tim Simenon, and me. There was already a serious group of people . . . maybe not directly running the label, but around. [We were] very productive . . . ideas were taken aboard and exploited, and obviously they [these ideas] were a big commercial success —S'Express and Bomb the Bass went to No. 1 in England [in 1988]. The idea was that it was an underground kind of label with a little bit more of an eye on commercial success.[8]

Throughout acid house's 1988–89 reign in London, and its enormous transformative effect on British culture, techno still found a way to remain relevant. May's Transmat label released the mind-blowing acid EP *All for Lee-sah* from Chicago artist K. Alexi Shelby, and Saunderson's KMS label contributed an acidic mix of the Wee Papa Girls' hit "Heat It Up (It's Like That)," for which he won a 1989 DMC award for best remix.[9] And though acid house nudged techno into the background to some degree, the "idea" of techno survived: the United Kingdom had been introduced to Detroit's music and was coming to accept its talents and personalities.

Belgium

While London embraced acid house and techno lingered in the background, a parallel scene was happening across the English Channel, in Belgium. As in England, early house and techno records had begun trickling in from the United States in the mid- to late 1980s, supplementing the huge diet of new wave records that sustained Belgium's club culture through 1988. This partially explains the advent of a new musical style called "new beat," an amalgamation of acid house structures with the slower pace and dramatics of European new wave.

For a time, there seemed to be great potential for increased interplay between the scenes in Detroit, London, and Ghent. The success of Saunderson's 1989 record "Rock to the Beat"—one of the starkest, bleakest techno records—fit perfectly with the slower new beat tempo, giving Saunderson a second international success independent of and parallel to that of "Big Fun." Says Rushton, "At the Haçienda [a club in Manchester], it ["Rock to the Beat"] was a huge house anthem. But it didn't really take off [in England], apart from in the north. What happened was that overseas—Belgium, Holland, and France—[people] got into the record and tried to license [it] from London. But [since] they couldn't . . . they all [recorded] their own versions of it."

According to journalist Joost DeLijser of Belgium's *Surreal Sound* magazine, new beat went a little too far in trying to expand its sound, squeezing out techno in the process. "The Belgian new beat labels monopolized the clubs as well as the major distribution channels, and it was hard to find U.S. records in Belgium," says DeLijser. "There were maybe three to five stores carrying what little got through." To complicate matters, there was an increasing proliferation of new beat compilations called *This Is New Beat* in the United States, released through Polygram Records. So Belgium wasn't getting any American records and Americans were getting too many of Belgium's. Other stumbling blocks included cultural and distribution-related gaps between the United States and Belgium—two issues that hadn't been problems in the U.S.-U.K. relationship.

Belgium was far from being the center of attention that London had become in the dance music world, and techno had yet to conquer its many obstacles. At the very least, however, Belgium gave the music a start on the Continent, familiarizing European audiences with the techno sound to come.

Dissonance

While techno struggled for acceptance in London and Belgium in the late 1980s, other English cities began relating to techno and acid house on a more basic level. In particular, the Northern Soul fans in cities like Birmingham, Sheffield, and Manchester seemed to recognize the loose connection Neil Rushton had drawn between Detroit's Motown past and its electronic future. In no small way, these fans would help connect England's general interest in soul music to the new electronic dance sounds coming from Detroit, creating a window of opportunity in an environment where techno was still treated as a mere offshoot of Chicago house. Says Rushton, "In the north of England, there had always been a following for soul records, especially from Detroit. That's why at the Haçienda, [DJ] Mike Pickering was playing the Detroit records before anyone in London. Like me, he'd grown up on this diet of soul music."

In fact, in 1988, aside from the concentrated bubble of energy and interest at Rhythm King, one had to travel outside London to Manchester to find Detroit records being played with any frequency. "The Haçienda really got behind those records," says Rushton. "In Manchester, you'd find all those records: 'Goodbye Kiss,' 'Groovin' without a Doubt,' 'Triangle of Love' —they were all revered. But in [London's] Spectrum on a Monday night, where you had 1,800 people, they weren't being played."

From the very beginning, Manchester's relationship with techno and acid house was bracketed by the city's position as a new wave and alternative mecca. Having spawned the Smiths, the Fall, and New Order, Manchester was a heavily band-oriented environment, offset by clubs like the Haçienda (which New Order helped fund). The most unique coming together occurred in Manchester's indie-rock scene, where bands like the Happy Mondays, the Stone Roses, and Inspiral Carpets took on some of the textures and/or lifestyle of acid house, dubbing their movement and the city "Madchester." Even for the unconverted, these bands created a kind of psychedelic sound that people could relate to, as well as a bridge to the more purist sounds of native bands 808 State and A Guy Called Gerald.

Thirty or so miles to the east, techno also connected with the city of Sheffield, reaching all the way back to the city's new wave idols (such as ABC and Heaven 17) and avant-gardists like Cabaret Voltaire. Sheffield had been reaching for soul and funk and feeling with electronic arms since the early 1980s. Detroit techno came at the right time—both to reignite the city's love for dance music and to legitimize the work of its own artists. The parallels between Detroit and Sheffield are numerous: struggles with an industrial base and near-fatal dependency on it, great musical traditions (Detroit's Motown and Sheffield's synth-pop), limited options for youth, and so on.

Two Sheffield natives, Rob Mitchell and Steve Beckett, had seen the connection a mile away; they were already collecting early output from Detroit and Chicago and had opened a record shop called Warp, spawning a label of the same name. Mitchell and Beckett also shared Cybotron's less-than-humble beginnings, selling ten thousand copies of their first release, Forgemasters' "Track with No Name." Their next several releases carried them out of the underground and, completely unexpectedly, into the U.K. Top 40.

Warp's third record, Sweet Exorcist's "Test One" (sometimes spelled "Testone" and pronounced "test tone"),[10] solidified Warp's success and defined Sheffield's techno sound. Released in 1990, "Test One" married the sounds of Yellow Magic Orchestra's 1980 classic "Computer Games" with a playful use of sampled dialogue from the film *Close Encounters of the*

Third Kind: "Is everybody ready on the dark side of the moon? Play the five tones." These two sentences led right into the song's punchy "bleep" sounds and frighteningly low-frequency bass rumble. Sheffield techno was stark, powerful, and playful—the perfect complement to Detroit techno's complex web of emotions.

Another component of the Sheffield scene—and one that would spread to other U.K. labels and artists—was the use of symbolic computer language. Musicians, bands, and events began hiding behind the signs, acronyms, and nomenclature of machines—years before the reign of the "@" sign and the digital revolution in music, communication, and commerce. Any random browse through a record shop's techno bin would have revealed names like 808 State, Electribe 101, LFO, Nexus 21, and so on.

The Detroit-Sheffield connection was commodified when Neil Rushton gathered artists from the two cities to appear side by side on *Biorhythm,* a series of two compilations released on Network Records in 1990. The *Biorhythm* liner notes, written by English music journalist John McCready, defined its sound as that "of outer London, a collection of mathematical modern music with bleeps," thus reinforcing the Sheffield aesthetic.

Another interesting development coinciding with the Sheffield "bleep" era was the group Orbital, formed by English brothers Phil and Paul Hartnoll in 1989. Hailing from a suburb southeast of London, the two took their name from the M25 orbital motorway that encircles the city. Orbital became the perfect assimilation of raw synthesized din, Detroit sentimentality, and raver spirituality—a process that began with a small run of one thousand copies of its first single, "Chime." "Chime" became a classic of rave crowds and attracted the attention of FFRR records, which signed the group to a multi-album deal.[11]

The artists north of and just outside London both complicated and simplified techno's original designs, shepherding it from 1988 to the biorhythms and bleeps of 1990. Most of these early sounds were strikingly original and carry the same emotional charge as listening to house or techno for the first time. There was an unspoken sense of establishment and accomplishment in the music—a sense that the United Kingdom was no longer dependent on records imported from Chicago and Detroit. These artists were also learning to address the dynamics of large crowds, which was becoming increasingly important as masses flocked to parties and raves across the country.

Losing Control

By the late 1980s, English dance parties had begun spreading beyond London-area clubs like Shoom, Spectrum, and the Trip and into open spaces (farms, warehouses, and even army depots). Free of the constraints of space and the law, parties grew into mass gatherings of thousands and became known as "raves." The term traces back at least as far as the "rave-ups" of the early 1970s—all-night dance parties within the Northern Soul subculture that started as an extension of 1960s "mod" culture. "Rave" was more than apt to describe the new phenomenon, even if the connection would be lost on most of its new participants.

As raves proliferated, acid house and techno merged with the usage and culture surrounding the drug ecstasy—a connection that seemed to happen overnight but had in fact followed a much more gradual path. Although illegal in Britain since 1977, ecstasy had been used by an insular crowd in the early and mid-1980s, with its heaviest concentration in the fashion and music industries. Most ecstasy usage at this time was still in small, intimate settings—groups of friends in homes and apartments.

Ecstasy use started changing as vacationing Brits came into contact with it on the island of Ibiza, off the coast of Spain. Usage swelled in Ibiza's hot and hedonistic environment, becoming part of the island's nightclub ritual and coinciding with some of the earliest house music imports from Chicago. By 1987, the blueprint for "ecstasy culture" was laid out in a style of dance music called Balearic (named for the group of islands to which Ibiza belongs). As vacationers dragged themselves back home to Britain's more isolated, chillier isles, they attempted to re-create the experience in local clubs. In acid house and techno, ecstasy users found the perfect music to match their hypersensory conditions. Likewise, techno now had legions of blissful Brits as fans—Brits who might otherwise have never set foot in a club or dance music shop. Unfortunately, the price on both sides was understanding.

When the British press caught wind of the acid house drug culture in 1988, it mistakenly publicized the drug of choice as LSD—no doubt basing its assumption on the acid house name. Either way, the concept that electronic dance music was inseparable from a chemically altered consciousness was constantly reinforced by both the uninformed and enthusiasts. Sensationalist fiction appeared in English newspapers and tabloids, written by reporters and editors who couldn't get past the word "acid" and the images it evoked. The British TV show *Top of the Pops* banned any song or band with the word "acid" in its name, and some radio entities censored even less discriminately. As Peter Ford recalls:

> They banned one of my records ["Chikki Chikki Ahh Ahh"] on Radio One. The refrain was "disco me to ecstasy," which of course was totally outrageous. It meant "to heaven"—there was no drug connection whatsoever in our minds when we wrote it. But of course they [the radio executives] immediately thought it was about drugs and banned it from Radio One! They went for the drug angle and made everybody aware of it. Then, of course, it [the drug angle] caught on really big-time [with the public].

The press was missing the point, focusing on the music's superficial novelty rather than its more interesting aspects, which were significantly changing the musical landscape. Says Ford, "It [acid house] wasn't so much about one instrument but more about basslines and atmospheres—and beats. It was more about an attitude . . . that you could make abstract sounds. Or you could approach the whole thing as an abstract thing—a piece of music that was mutated by 303 or a house/acid track. That was the exciting thing about it."

The negative connotations of "acid" became as troubling to Detroit's techno artists as they were to the English establishment. Drugs were almost completely absent in Detroit's techno scene, small as it was, and the artists were undoubtedly a bit shocked to find their music fused with any kind of drug-related experience. The Music Institute didn't even serve alcohol, only juice and water. "I've never seen such a group of teetotalers—no one drank and no one took drugs," notes Sarah Gregory. Some, like May, were immediately and vocally at odds with techno's association with drug culture, and especially with those within the dance music community who helped perpetuate it. Following the surge in Detroit's crack cocaine sales through the early and mid-1980s, and the lives lost as a result, drugs had become a much more serious matter to techno's producers. For them, drugs carried deadly connotations.

May became especially incensed at the 1989 New Music Seminar in New York City, where he and house music producer Marshall Jefferson stormed out of a panel discussion called "Wake Up America, You're Dead." Many members of the panel were producers from England's indie-rock scene, which had itself become intertwined with the emerging rave culture. Before an audience made up largely of young hopefuls, Happy Mondays' producer Nathan McGough admitted that his band had unguarded connections to drugs and criminal activity. Says May, "He didn't realize that . . . the few frivolous words he said would last longer in these kids' minds. When I asked him if they [the Happy Mondays] were a bunch of drug dealers, he said yes. He said yes! I hate to say it, but some kid may get killed through shit like that, you never know."[12]

Raves had a radical effect on techno and acid house music, which were being exposed to larger and larger crowds, some numbering in the thousands. For DJs at these events, the challenge was to alter their sets to match the "heightened" state of the audience. Heightened serotonin levels called for records (or portions thereof) that had only the most dramatic and energetic qualities—literally the *ecstatic* moments. There were already a good number of them about—Rhythim Is Rhythim's "Strings of Life" and Mr. Fingers' "Can You Feel It," for example—but the supply was still limited at this early stage. Exactly what comprised a "rave" record was as yet unclear.

What *was* clear was that music journalists were having a hard time covering the new music scene, struggling between judging techno and its ilk for their functionality and for their purely artistic merit. In this arena, much of Detroit's musical innovation went undetected—especially that of Derrick May and Carl Craig. Critics argued that conceptual epics like Rhythim Is Rhythim's "The Beginning" took too long to get to the point. The crowd was rocking the music, not the other way around.

Frontierland

In 1991 raves finally crossed the Atlantic and began exploring America's "wide-open spaces." Detroit lost its exclusive claim to being the country's only techno capital,[13] and scenes expanded in New York, Dallas, Los Angeles, and San Francisco. Thus began techno's ironic existence as an import in the country that had supplied the music in the first place. And, in some part because of this interlude between techno's genesis in Detroit and its return to the United States, a schism formed between American audiences and the original house and techno producers.

Most of Detroit's and Chicago's finest DJs and producers had averaged about twenty-five years of age when they first touched down in London in

1988. By the time Americans were introduced to raves some four years later, these pioneers were thirty or older. In the meantime, no one had been servicing the club circuits back home. The aging African American audience of techno's past had gone back underground, to smallish close-knit house parties in local halls—ironically, very much like those of its high school days. By the time techno and house DJs began getting booked in the United States again, they faced significant culture and generation gaps. The rave culture had become a youth-oriented movement, centering on primarily white kids less than eighteen years of age, and the old concept of a DJ's "children" took on a literal meaning.

Putting this predicament and the dangers of teen drug use aside, there are positive aspects to the development of America's rave landscape. First, its participants took their enthusiasm for house and techno with them as they graduated from high school and college, eventually becoming consumers with more disposable income. Before the collapse of the CD-based music industry aside, the so-called electronica niche became a bit more than a niche. Second, raves inspired a generation of DJs toward new levels of creativity. Support mechanisms and networks across the country created a generation for which raves were much more natural than they could ever be for techno's pioneers or even for the first generation of British enthusiasts. It might be far-fetched to assume that an entire generation of party-goers took up apprenticeships, but advances in digital mixing capabilities have democratized the art somewhat. For now, the reality of kids in America's heartland buying Technics 1200 turntables or Ableton Live software and developing "hand/ear coordination" is promising enough.

The oddest characteristics of American raves were the country's nooks and crannies, which became part of the greater scene. While big cities and college towns served as hubs, hundreds of "pocket universes" existed between them. From the southwest corner of the country to Oklahoma City to resort areas in the Poconos, raves proliferated independently of northern urban centers. Even stranger is the distance ravers traveled to follow events, which were sometimes two or three states apart.

It's a shame that this scene didn't live on indefinitely as the twenty-first-century equivalent of the Deadheads or even Phish's phans or phriends, but ambitious lawmakers caught up with the alternate universe and economies of rave in the name of fighting the abuse of ecstasy. In fact, then senator Joseph Biden sponsored the RAVE (Reducing Americans' Vulnerability to Ecstasy) Act in 2002, making it a crime for an owner of a venue to knowingly open it up to events where illegal drugs are used. The original bill did not pass, but a similar one (the Illicit Drug Anti-Proliferation Act) made it through in 2003, and has in essence destroyed the entire scene in the name of the War on Drugs.

But techno outlasted the rise and fall of rave, as inseparable as many critics thought the two entities. Before raves hit U.S. shores, techno music went through painful changes as its base grew wider and more diverse. And attempting to make the same jump to American mainstream culture (versus the rave subculture) was a frightening thought. Instead, the nurturing environment of creative, close-knit local scenes has been the general trend, and has been largely successful. Unanswered questions remain about whether raves will ever be reconciled with U.S. club culture. As the rave movement reached critical mass in the United Kingdom, this question was answered by the British government, which passed licensing legislation that in effect prohibited the ravers' mass gatherings, forcing the remaining diehards to roam the countryside in nomadic packs. Techno and acid house had reached the upper limits of scale in Britain, collapsing back into the guest lists and sexual politics of nightclubs. It just took a while for this to happen in the United States.

So where did all of this transformation leave Detroit? In three short years, northern England had shepherded acid house and techno through 1988's "Summer of Love" and into the massive exposure of 1990. Acid house, like its pharmaceutical namesake, had taken ravers to a sweltering high of excitement and interest in dance music. And, rather than crash on the way down, ravers were finding solace in the rhythms of techno, which had quietly outlasted its trippy cousin. So how did a comparatively sleepy Midwestern city relate to this movement of global proportions?

At first, Detroit's creative strata had no answer. Translating techno back into its original "language" after three years of exposure to rave culture was a near impossibility. But instead of dwelling on how far removed they had become, Detroit's artists decided to change the rules a second time. The answers did finally come — in a fierce musical reassertion and a new generation of world-beaters.

5

Off to Battle

Redefining the
Detroit Underground,
1990–1995

By 1991, after three years in the U.K. spotlight, techno had been mutated,
co-opted, and just plain misunderstood. The rave movement's economies
of scale had drastically altered the genre, sapping its music of complexity,
intimacy, and soul. While some Detroit artists continued to try to find a
place in the established industry, the Detroit sound as a whole went back
"underground," reacting with creative approaches and new business mod-
els. In the process, these artists made the underground a viable economic
entity with its own means of production, distribution, and promotion, and,
above all, an emphasis on integrity over accessibility.

Many Detroit artists had tired of chasing after deals in the United States.
Larger, more enthusiastic audiences were just across the Atlantic and were
branching out all over the world. (Not until 1993–94 did Detroit's artists connect with the American rave scene.) This created a dilemma for Atkins, May,

and Saunderson, already deified by the music press as "the Belleville Three," "the Big Three" (in lieu of the "Big Three" Detroit automakers), or even "the Holy Trinity." High praise indeed—but while it kept their day planners filled with European bookings, it also left less and less time to run their respective record labels or to develop new artists, of which there seemed to be more than anyone had ever expected. Instead of becoming embittered, however, these newcomers took the hint and started their own labels instead.

This next wave of labels quickly established distinct identities, greater than and separate from the sum of the artists' personalities.[2] Walking the tightrope of anonymity and instant recognition was the great skill these artists contributed to Detroit techno. And despite recurring bouts of infighting and misunderstandings, they hung together much as the first three labels had done, paving the way musically and organizationally for all those to follow.

Though the Music Institute had closed in 1989, unable to keep its sophisticated approach alive in an unsophisticated Detroit downtown, more established clubs like the Shelter and the Majestic kept techno flowing through their sound systems into the early 1990s. The Majestic was home to Blake Baxter, a skilled DJ who painted a broad palette of dance music styles for the equally diverse Friday night crowd. Everything from acid house and S'Express to Section 25's hazy industrial classic "Looking from a Hilltop" bounced around the Majestic's cavernous interior.

Closer to the Detroit River (which separates Detroit from Windsor, Ontario) was the Shelter, situated in the basement of St. Andrew's Hall, a former Scottish social club and home to alternative concerts since 1980. This is where, after waiting through a rotation of numerous local DJs, an eighteen-year-old talent named Richie Hawtin finally got his chance to build a crowd.

Approach and Identify

Richie Hawtin was only ten years old when he moved with his family from the tiny English village of Middleton-Cheney to Windsor, a city in the extreme southernmost part of Ontario, Canada (so much so that it wraps under and is actually south of Detroit). Hawtin remembers: "I remember getting off the plane and seeing all these wires. [It was] the first thing we all noticed, because in England most of the telephone and power wires are underground. The only pictures we had seen of Canada had been of bears, hills, and mountains, and we got off in the flattest place we had ever been to—concrete and wires everywhere. My mum was in hysterics, saying, 'What have we done?' It was crazy."

Once an outgoing kid, Hawtin's new environs made him an alien of sorts. "When I came here it really, really changed my character," says Hawtin. "I became a lot more withdrawn, a lot shier, and more like the person I am now. People used to tell me 'It would be cool to have your English accent' [but] . . . that was the thing I wanted to get rid of most. I just wanted to be assimilated and be like everyone else."

By the time he was just out of high school, Hawtin had found at least one way to adapt: through music. Hawtin began his DJ career in Windsor when he was only sixteen or seventeen years old, as a logical extension of his and his friends' love of music. Somehow Hawtin became the "designated DJ," stumbling into the role by default. Hawtin recalls:

> A lot of kids my age and younger from Windsor really wanted to hear that alternative electronic stuff, but no one could really hear it out. I remember going down to this club and saying, "I'd really like to do a night here—just a one-off.[3] Can we rent this place?" I was just haggling with the club owner, [but I] walked out of there with a DJ job. I was going to be the one [spinning] at this party, but I really wasn't a DJ yet. I didn't know what I was getting into.

Eventually Hawtin began landing gigs in Detroit, working his way up the ladder in the city's nightlife circuit, where there were at least three notable vacancies following the first *Techno!* compilation in 1988. By 1989, Hawtin's night at the Shelter became known as "Confusion," mushrooming in size and scope to pull in diverse crowds, interracial couples, and, above all, money. Like Baxter at the Majestic, Hawtin helped expand techno's audience, bringing it to the area's students and adventurous clubbers from the suburbs. By this time, Hawtin had already begun thinking about translating his energy and skill into sound recordings, having become friends with Shelter regular and Detroit native Kenny Larkin. As Hawtin remembers, "Kenny was this crazy guy who used to dance around screaming, 'Richie Rich, Richie Rich, Richie Rich!'[4] We used to drive around listening to Derrick May mix tapes, and we did some messing around at my house trying to hook up an old Korg keyboard to an Amiga computer!"

Necessary Elements

The Shelter is also where Hawtin met John Acquaviva, a DJ from London, Ontario, who had become interested in the Detroit scene. Like Hawtin, Acquaviva is a European transplant, having moved as a child to Canada from a small village in the foothills of southern Italy. Being six years older than Hawtin, Acquaviva had a longer and more eclectic DJ history. At one point in the late 1980s, he was known for fast hip-hop style mixes—much like the Jeff Mills "Wizard" style of old—in which songs would be pitched up as high as the turntables would allow. Flyers would commonly list Acquaviva as "J'acquaviva +8," the contracted name a reference to "jack" (a Chicago slang term for house music), and the numerical addition designating his preferred turntable pitch setting.

Acquaviva and Hawtin started trying to break into the more established Detroit labels, especially Derrick May's Transmat. Like Saunderson and Atkins, however, May was either too busy or not interested, and the two had little success. They decided to take matters into their own hands and, in 1990, borrowed the "+8" from Acquaviva's DJ moniker to form the perfect symbol for their new record label. Plus 8 released its first record, "Elements of Tone," later that year.

Recorded by Hawtin and Acquaviva as the States of Mind ensemble, "Elements of Tone" was a clever song built around samples from the low-tech Merlin toy (essentially an electronic game of "magic square"). With its unapologetic computer noises, "Elements of Tone" linked Plus 8 to the Sheffield "bleep" trend, expanding the definition of "Detroit" techno beyond its geographical borders.

At this point Kenny Larkin, who had worked with Hawtin in States of Mind before Acquaviva came onboard, began working separately with Acquaviva. The two recorded Plus 8's second release, "We Shall Overcome," later that year under Larkin's own name. Larkin would eventually ease into the science fiction nomenclature common to techno, but at this stage he seemed more concerned with terrestrial matters, such as the song's Martin Luther King samples.[5] Perhaps "We Shall Overcome" was an unconscious call for tolerance, as Plus 8's next marketing move would be poorly received among the largely African American techno community in Detroit.

For the white label of their third release later that year, the members of Plus 8 had the words "The Future Sound of Detroit" stamped in red on the back. But while they had intended this statement to project an idea of Detroit techno as a large regional sound, it ended up having the opposite effect—many Detroit artists felt that Plus 8 was cashing in on a reputation it hadn't yet earned. "That's why we had some problems when we started Plus 8," says Hawtin. "It wasn't that we were trying to jump onto that scene. . . . [Going to Detroit] was just like getting in my car and going down the street. . . . I just happened to get out an extra two dollars to get there. I didn't see it as a different place." The fact that Hawtin and Acquaviva were among the first white techno artists in the Detroit area didn't help either, and the white label's stamp raised the ire of Detroit's African American techno community that, in general, remained suspicious of Plus 8 for years afterward.

Ironically, the greenhorn mistake that isolated Plus 8 also became one of its biggest successes; when officially released as "Technarchy" later that year (1990), the single sold around twenty thousand copies. "Technarchy" had an aggressive synth line, growling out of an old Pro-One analog keyboard.[6] Though there were similar compositions out at the time, such as 808 State's "Cubik," "Technarchy" marked the point at which Plus 8 stopped following trends and began setting them. As Acquaviva recalls:

> That one record really got the world interested. Richie [Hawtin] was already in top form as a DJ and he edited the song together. . . . We had done a handful of mixes and Richie took them, chopped them up, and said, "I've been to parties and this is going to work . . . this is how it should be." When Dan [techno artist Daniel Bell] and I heard it, we said, "You know what? We sound as good as the records we buy!" We were so proud of ourselves.

The group behind "Technarchy" was Cybersonik, a collaboration formed earlier that year by Hawtin and a like-minded acquaintance from the Shelter, Daniel Bell. Born in Sacramento, California, to a Canadian father and American mother, Bell had moved to Canada when he was two years old. From there, his family had moved frequently, eventually settling in St. Catharine's, Ontario, just outside Niagara. It seems a bit unusual that he, Hawtin, Acquaviva, and Larkin would all meet at the Shelter, especially given the seven-hour bus ride from the Toronto area down to Detroit, but Bell points to their uncommon common ground as an explanation. "When you talk to people in music, I think a lot of them had a point in their life when they felt isolated," he says. "Music was very important to them because it was something consistent in their life."

Plus 8's musicians and producers soon stretched far beyond Windsor, London, and the Niagara peninsula. The label's next collaborator was Jochem Paap, an aspiring musician and DJ from the Netherlands, a country that was quickly catching up to England and Belgium in terms of its enthusiasm for techno. Paap had discovered Plus 8 in its first year of development, a testament to how quickly techno was disseminating through Europe at the time. According to Hawtin:

> Right after "+8001" and "+8002" [Plus 8's first two releases], [Paap] called us and we did a small radio interview for a Dutch station he was working for. Then John [Acquaviva] and he started to talk, and he [Paap] mentioned that he did music and would be interested to see what we thought. He sent us a ninety-minute tape which blew us away. We put out the first record ["Wicked Saw," released in 1991] and then later on we flew him over to hang out in Windsor and Detroit. That's where he first recorded "Pull Over" [in 1991].

Like Acquaviva, Paap was known for a fast hip-hop mixing style—so fast that his DJ moniker was "Speedy J." Speedy J rounded out the Plus 8 identity, which was becoming increasingly complex and global. As Acquaviva recalls:

> Our first logo was kind of a flag—we've always been into our little country, our little empire or whatever, and [along with other new labels] we were people that finally picked up the baton from Kevin, Juan, and Derrick and added to the dimension of Detroit. [But] we got so much flak [for that], and were so pissed, that our second logo was . . . the Plus 8 world on its axis with Detroit, Windsor, Toronto, London, Ontario, and Rotterdam listed—we had artists from [each of] these cities. We kind of put our tails between our legs and said we shouldn't push the fact [of being from the Detroit area], because obviously our presence was upsetting a lot of people.

By the time Plus 8 released its first compilation, *From Our Minds to Yours, Vol. 1,* in mid-1991, the label had grown considerably—not in the size of its roster but in dealing with its early faux pas and with larger entities overseas. Wide-eyed enthusiasm and raw talent had given these artists a great start, but their learned business sense and ingrained worldview would become critical for lasting success.

Like the first Detroit techno compilation, which was recorded by just a handful of artists using various pseudonyms, *From Our Minds to Yours* had its share of padding: Hawtin was involved with seven of the ten tracks on vinyl (and ten of the thirteen on CD). Still, there was enough exclusive material (including a remix of "Technarchy") to establish Plus 8 as a solid label with designs on more than a week-to-week cycle of twelve-inch singles. The compilation was also the very first techno product from the Detroit area to be released in all three configurations (vinyl, cassette, and CD), thanks in part to the U.K. label Champion, with which Plus 8 had signed a licensing deal. Unfortunately, according to Hawtin, Champion wasn't interested in a long-term relationship. "It didn't take us too long to realize that things were fucked up," he says. "As soon as [the product] came out and we started to ask for sales figures, etc., they became increasingly harder to contact."

Despite its behind-the-scenes instability, *From Our Minds to Yours* was a landmark event for Plus 8, and its artists began positioning themselves for the opportunities that followed. The label embarked on its first tour in 1991, mostly centered around dates in the United Kingdom and featuring Cybersonik, F.U.S.E.,[7] and Speedy J—all of the Plus 8 artists with sizable hits at the time. Larkin was left behind in Detroit, which naturally didn't sit well with the label's only African American artist.

With tensions high between Larkin and the rest of Plus 8, Larkin moved out and moved on. He eventually recorded as Dark Comedy for May's Transmat label in 1992 and positioned himself as a premier solo artist more in sync with album-length projects, such as those coming out on the English label Warp and the Belgian label R&S. Larkin's landmark 1994 album *Azimuth,* released on Warp in the United Kingdom and TVT in the United States, was the first domestically released Detroit techno album (outside of those released by the more pop-oriented Inner City) to feature an artist on its cover.

Perhaps because of their science fiction moniker, or simply because it was easier to market white electronic musicians, Cybersonik's Hawtin and Bell started attracting the attention of a few U.S. independents. One of them, Chicago's Wax Trax label, saw Cybersonik as a possible complement to its stable of unruly industrial dance artists. Although the two declined to sign with the label, Wax Trax's interest surprised Hawtin and Bell, who realized that their sound was being perceived as much more aggressive than they'd intended.

This insight was further reinforced on a visit to Rotterdam in 1992. There, Bell, Hawtin, and Acquaviva came face to face with the "dark side" of techno, one that Cybersonik had only hinted at and toyed with in its music. Rotterdam's Parkzicht club had earned a reputation as the Netherlands' most hard-core club. Along with DJ selections skewed toward noise, the turntables at the Parkzicht were rigged to pitch up records to +15 (almost double Plus 8's namesake speed), creating a frenetic pace of up to 200 bpm (beats per minute) and creating an ominous, apocalyptic sound.

As the Plus 8 crew discovered, the Parkzicht crowd often latched onto songs like Cybersonik's "Thrash," and even its drums-only instrumental version, "Thrash Beats," and was using them in ways the group could never have imagined. A cross-section of the Parkzicht faithful were also soccer fans and had begun fusing their love of hard-core techno with a soccer rivalry between their local Rotterdam team and that of Amsterdam. The Rotterdam fans, who had a history of chanting "Joden! Joden!" ("Jews, Jews!" in Dutch) at the Amsterdam team (which was historically supported by Amsterdam's predominantly Jewish entrepreneurial class), began rallying their stadium chant in the Parkzicht, seemingly spurred by the "Thrash" chorus of "Join! Join!" (a snippet of the "Join in the chant!" chorus from English industrial outfit Nitzer Ebb's song of the same name).

It was clear that Plus 8 wasn't going to follow the degradation of "jack" to "jack-boot" and, stunned by the Parkzicht experience, the label backed away from Cybersonik's sonic fury. "Those tracks [the harder ones like "Thrash"] sound really rigid now," says Hawtin. "We liked machine-driven music, but we didn't like it so rigid—that was the difference with Detroit music. None of us were making hard music just for the sake of it. . . . We weren't slamming people over the head just for the sake of it. It was just intense."

At around the same time Plus 8's sub-label Probe was launched,[8] in 1991, Cybersonik ceased to exist, with its last release ("Jackhammer/Machine Gun") featuring Bell and Hawtin on sides A and B, respectively. Hawtin's and Bell's interests were beginning to pull them in different directions, and by the time the group ended, they both thought Cybersonik's line of experimentation silly, if not potentially dangerous.

After leaving the group, Hawtin became increasingly interested and adept in the studio. Beginning with releases as F.U.S.E. and Circuit Breaker, he continued his experiments as "Plastikman," with a four-album arc released by Plus 8 between 1993 and 1998, and a comeback in 2003. Though it seemed as if Hawtin's new guise was simply a shift from one cartoon character to another (from Richie Rich to the pliable hero Plastic Man), the name was more a descriptive term for the rubbery, experimental sounds coming out of his pair of Roland TB-303s. Perhaps a reaction to both the overload of hard core and heavy usage of the 303, the Plastikman sound was decidedly slower and more atmospheric, yet still every bit as intense as first-generation acid house and techno. Plastikman was also one of Plus 8's best-selling artists, building a loyal base of listeners and party-goers around great music, a simplistic logo, and some extraneous ks in his track titles ("Kriket," "Helikopter," and so forth). Assisted by a recurring relationship with Nova-Mute (a sub-label of Mute), Hawtin's Plastikman project steadily carved out a niche with North American audiences.

By 1992, the stylized world pictured in Plus 8's logo was being made increasingly real by a growing complement of artists, who were all spinning off in very different directions. In addition to Speedy J, fellow Netherlander V-Room (Gijs Vroom) signed on, as did Germany's Sysex (Heinrich Tillack) and an up-and-coming Japanese techno artist named Ken Ishii, who recorded under the pseudonym UTU. American techno artists also gravitated to Plus 8, including Joey Bertram, who recorded with Hawtin as Vortex, and ex–Psychic TV member Fred Gianelli, who had collaborated earlier with Hawtin and Bell in a group called Spawn.[9]

The Detroit Experiment

Another group of Hawtin's collaborators were not artists per se but the paragon of Detroit party promoters. Known these days through their efforts with Paxahau (the production force behind "Movement: Detroit's Electronic Music Festival"), Sam Fotias and Jason Huvaere were then part of the core team that made Plus 8 "parties" and dozens of other events happen.

That's right: the word "rave" never took hold with the same force in the Motor City as it did in other parts of the world. As they would prove out over the first half of the 1990s, Detroit's underground events had as much distinct character as the music that inspired them. As the Midwest tends not to be the same kind of sponge for imported phenomena, the lag in rave culture hitting Detroit turned out to be better for the scene.

Without as much emphasis on the trappings of the subculture, this generation of Detroit parties drew inspiration from the music, and in some way the physical reality of the city. Jason Huvaere, now the president of Paxahau Promotions Group LLC, remembers this connection as being strong from the start: "Without sounding too new-agey or metaphysical, I think that Detroit, the actual location of Detroit, is the instigator behind everything."

In a tangible sense, it was *where* the parties were thrown: the Packard Plant, the Bankle Building on Woodward, Roma Hall on Gratiot. There was something beyond just the opportunistic grabbing of available space —a combination of adventure and a respect that swelled into pride for the city. Making the "ruins" of Detroit come alive one party at a time might sound like a superficial, suburban, infidel mentality, but there was a collective effect. Though motivated by a love for the music, this generation of promoters was sustained by a need to give Detroit and its artists the outlets they had been without for so many decades.

Many, like Huvaere, ended up moving to the city and even living in some of the spaces that housed the parties. One improbable example was 1217 Griswold, made up of ten run-down loft spaces. For a few years, Detroit artists and promoters inhabited seven of them and hosted dozens of visiting rave-fugees from all over the Midwest. John "Bileebob" Williams was an aspiring DJ whose loft sat on top of the burned-out Restaurant Du Soleil on the street level.

> There were 15 to 17 of us living there between 1993 and '94. Maybe two or three of us had credible 9 to 5 jobs. The creative spirit of that building and the brotherhood that was cemented continues to thrive in the current underground. Most notably, the seeds of Paxahau were planted in Jason Huvaere's blue loft space. It had a win-dowed office and was the perfect setup for things to come. My roommate, Alan Bogl, was one of the founding members of the legendary promotion group Voom. Voom was the cornerstone of Detroit's early rave scene and set the precedent for the way Detroit after-hours events should be thrown and hosted. [And] within a year I had lived among some of the most creative promoters and underground fixtures including Nancy Mitchell, Jon Santos, Dean Major and Leto.[10]

With this network of promoters (which also included "Blackbx," "Syst3m," and Dat Duong and Brian Gillespie's "Poor Boy") behind them, the DJs and artists who weren't Derrick May, Kevin Saunderson, and Juan Atkins had a real way to build their audiences. Richie Hawtin was the obvious example, as he threw several parties with his Plus 8 label's imprint on all of them. But there were up-and-coming talents such as Derek Plaslaiko (who DJed with Adriel Thornton's Tribe 9), as well as mainstays of the scene like Carl Craig, Mike Huckaby, and Darrell Wynn — or just "D Wynn." Says Huvaere: "D Wynn never made the cut like the others and was a totally unique kind of DJ. He had this chug-chug way of mixing techno and house that would make people crazy on the dance floor."

This was the Detroit underground's major aftershock. The initial explosion of techno had quickly spread overseas and the original artists followed to a large extent. This next movement had even more DIY and grassroots elements to it than before, a close-knit identity that still exists somewhere in the heart of the scene. "I went out to every party I possibly could," says Plaslaiko. "At the time, promoters *took turns* with their Saturdays so there weren't really choices of parties to hit on a weekend. This time was sacred."

Though it was still a small scene, and always will be by comparison to top-tier markets, the community grew. It wasn't a widespread thing, but the roots ran deep. And it wasn't merely a by-product or an accident alongside techno — the music community was establishing itself in its own right and was now starting to give back. According to Huvaere, "Regionally, that's where Detroit's reputation came from, 1993 to 1995. That's where everyone came in and experienced these events. You couldn't duplicate them — they never got busted and they always went into the next day. People went home *limping*."

Covert Action

Wedged between the Music Institute on one end and the boom in Detroit party culture a few years later, you had Carl Craig, a former protégé of Derrick May. In the fall of 1990, he returned to Detroit from an extended "residency" in England, bringing with him a new perspective and DATs (digital audio tapes) full of material, including the remains of a failed Sarah Gregory project on Rhythm King. Craig also brought back a sound he had been developing in London, one that jumped light years ahead of the marker set by Plus 8's first release, "Elements of Tone," earlier that year. By combining breakbeats, vocals, and noisy, gravelly samples with an uncanny sense of melody and timing, Craig established himself as one of the most

CARL CRAIG OF PLANET E COMMUNICATIONS.
(Doug Coombe)

innovative artists in the genre. Unfortunately, few outside Detroit would give his experimentation the exposure or recognition it deserved.

Craig chose two new pseudonyms to reflect his new sound: BFC and Psyche.[11] Keeping with his Transmat roots, Craig used BFC to help kick off the new Transmat sub-label, Fragile, in 1989, while Psyche's *Crackdown* EP became Transmat's twelfth release in 1990. Both records featured colorful op art graphics that matched up perfectly with Craig's new direction and broke with Detroit's tradition of more utilitarian labels (if it was possible to have a tradition at this early stage). As for his remaining material,

Craig had other plans, having bandied about the idea of starting a new label with friend Damon Booker, a fellow Detroiter who had been helping Art Payne with promotions at Saunderson's KMS Records. But the new label would have to wait: in 1989, Craig became part of Derrick May's Rhythim Is Rhythim and traveled with the group on its European tour. In the meantime, Booker continued to DJ for Windsor radio station CJAM in a time slot called "House Factor," all the while planning the debut of his and Craig's new label.

Like Plus 8, Booker's and Craig's new label would get its start in bedrooms and basements. (Plus 8's Hawtin had even dubbed his studio "UTK" for "Under the Kitchen.") As Booker recalls, there was a unique thread among Detroit techno's second group of self-starters—the uncharacteristic patience of their parents.

> My grandmother never complained about how much noise we made in the base-
> ment, and his [Craig's] parents never complained about how much noise we
> made in his bedroom—and his bedroom was right next to theirs. We'd be in
> there [at] 12:30 or 1:00 in the morning, and Carl would have those JBLs pumpin'!
> He had the Prophet [keyboard] and a sampler in there . . . and at my house we'd
> be listening to records or Carl would be making a tape until 1:00 or 2:00 in the
> morning. [Their patience] is one of the things that contributed to our success.

The new label, called Retroactive, officially came onto the scene in 1990 with a compilation called *Equinox,* yet another conceptual follow-up to the earlier *Techno!* series. *Equinox* was essentially a collection of the Detroit talent waiting in the wings, from Sherard Ingram's Urban Tribe project to the early rumblings of Underground Resistance (UR) and Octave One.[12] In a sense, Booker and Craig had put to vinyl a preview of the next two years of Detroit techno—a subtle declaration that its sound could no longer be defined simply by the productions of Atkins, May, and Saunderson. Of the sounds on *Equinox,* Craig recalls:

> UR went on a very arranged level [and] the structures were more song-based.
> It was a good combination because it was a musician and a DJ that were work-
> ing together on the production. They had the right elements to sell the records.
> [Octave One] had their thing happening which was maybe more "light techno,"
> a kind of "housey" thing that was more instrumentally oriented. And then you

had me, just trying to make anything that was different than everyone else's stuff! What we were all doing was showing that there was a different concept to techno than what you [were already hearing].

The Retroactive label came at a crucial time for Detroit techno—when KMS and Metroplex were idle, bordering on inactive. Saunderson's and Atkins's early successes and attention to the European market had left their pioneering labels neglected, and there were even rumors of the two labels closing for good. Transmat had been able to maintain a respectable, although slowed, existence; though his own material wasn't being pressed up, Derrick May had only to flex his A&R muscle or use his keen DJ ears to make something happen. Transmat latched onto several records that were already or were destined to become hits, like Joey Beltram's "Energy Flash" in 1990 and 3 Phase's "Der Klang Der Familie" in 1992.

Though Plus 8 had stepped up first, Retroactive proved perhaps a more inspirational label, with Craig providing a logical and physical link to Transmat and Rhythim Is Rhythim. To some degree, anticipation for new Transmat records spilled over into Retroactive releases, including Inertia's "Nowhere to Run" (a disguised side project of [A Guy Called] Gerald Simpson), and the classics "Throw" by the Paperclip People and "Never on Sunday" by Octave One (all released in 1991).

Within a year, conflicting schedules and periodic fallouts between Craig and Booker resulted in the disbanding of Retroactive. Booker continued to DJ in Germany as DJ Blackout, introducing artists like Ohio's Dan Curtin on his short-lived Sinewave 33 1/3 label, while Craig went on to push the envelope of experimental dance music under his new imprint, Planet E. Formed in 1992, Planet E has survived to develop a roster as diverse as its proprietor's tastes, including an ever-evolving techno/jazz project called Innerzone Orchestra, the hybrid house music of Moodymann, and the next-generation amalgams of Recloose.

Message to the Majors
Owing to its uniqueness as a music form, techno has flourished in the worldwide underground community—with "underground" being the operative word. In the past, this term has been used to describe music that simply didn't make it to the airwaves or into retail chains. By the early 1990s, however, "underground" had become a statement of purpose. And for

some Detroit techno artists, going underground meant total retrenchment. This effort to restore techno's lost information, putting the focus back on Detroit and the fundamentals of its music, became the sole occupation of one group and one label: Underground Resistance (UR).

UR was a stroke of genius that evolved from simple collaborations between a couple of guys who spent a lot of time in recording studios—one an ex-session musician (Mike Banks) and the other a well-known and respected DJ (Jeff Mills). Like most other Detroit techno artists, both came from the northwest side, though they wouldn't actually meet until 1989 in Detroit's United Sound recording studio on Second Avenue.

In addition to his famed role as a talented technical DJ, Mills came to the relationship with a more recent background in "industrial" music (also called "industrial dance").[13] In 1989 and 1990, nightclub denizens who weren't listening to techno were listening to the rigid sounds of industrial, its basslines quantized into rapid-fire stabs. There were dozens of European acts that came to define industrial music and its scene, from England's Nitzer Ebb to Canada's Skinny Puppy and Front Line Assembly. Coinciding with its new beat phenomenon, Belgium also spawned a number of influential industrial acts, chief among them the Brussels band Front 242, formed in 1981. Front 242's material was as stark and foreboding as dance music could be, but briefly warmed up to a more crossover sound with 1988's *Front by Front* and the 1989 EP *Never Stop.*[14]

One of the American hubs of industrial was Chicago, home to Ministry, Die Warzau, My Life with the Thrill Kill Kult, and the Wax Trax record label.[15] Similar to the techno/house relationship, Detroit took direction from Chicago in establishing its own industrial scene, outlined by the four-man outfit Code Industry (née Code Assault) and the Final Cut,[16] a collaboration between Mills and Tony Srock. Code Industry was unique in that it was industrial's only all-African American group; Mills's involvement with the Final Cut, however, is far more intriguing for the purposes of this discussion.

Instead of taking the logical route and taking his DJ skills to the hip-hop community, Mills began his recording career in the comparatively unfunky genre of industrial. In 1989, Mills and Srock formed the Final Cut as a sort of backup band for the group True Faith, a more pop- or house-styled dance outfit featuring the vocals of Bridgett Grace. Together, the two groups released a handful of records, including "You Can't Deny the Bass" and "Take Me Away" on Jerry Capaldi's Paragon Records.[17] Perhaps because of Capaldi's position as executive producer of Paragon (as opposed to the autonomous, artist-run settings of Metroplex, Transmat, and KMS), several artists (including those in the Final Cut) had a falling out with Capaldi, contributing early on to a distrust between black and white techno artists and producers.

Hawtin remembers the negative dynamics at Paragon well, as they fed into the stigma following Plus 8 after its "Future Sound of Detroit" error. "Around that time there was a real problem with Paragon," he says. "There were a couple of bad deals [that left] a bad taste in people's mouths . . . some people ripping other people off . . . and it happened to be suburban white people coming in and doing that. . . . It got into that classic stereotype of the white guy taking over the black guy's turf." Though the problems with Paragon are largely forgotten, and Plus 8 has survived most of the criticism hurled its way, this dormant tension between black and white artists still exists in techno.

After Paragon, the Final Cut began to realize its potential, drawing inspiration from the industrial sounds of Chicago and Belgium (where industrial dance music was known as "electronic body music" or "EBM") and crossbreeding them with the native techno sound. This amazing hybrid was best captured on the 1990 release *Deep into the Cut* on Big Sex/Interfisch Records, a German label best known as home to the sinister sounds of Sheffield's Clock DVA.

Interfisch was the by-product of a kind of dadaist German think tank called Fischbüro, started in the mid-1980s by Dimitri Hegemann, who was disenchanted with the suicide rock scene in Berlin. Interfisch faded from sight by 1991,[18] but not before coinciding with another project Hegemann was involved with: the Atonal festivals (usually given the German pronunciation "Ah-tone-ahhl"). These festivals were explorations and celebrations of noise and sound, and the last one featured the Final Cut alongside early English techno luminaries like 808 State and Baby Ford.

By 1990–91, the Final Cut had fallen under the direction of Srock, who steered the project more toward rock 'n' roll. This was similar to the direction many industrial groups of the day were moving in (Ministry, Nitzer Ebb, and so forth), all incorporating guitar to varying extremes. After one last twelve-inch single bearing the Mills influence ("I Told You Not to Stop" in 1990), the Final Cut aimed directly for the industrial genre and the audiences of the Canadian label Nettwerk, which released the Final Cut's second album, *Consumed,* in 1991. Despite some clever layering of samples and expanded vocal treatments, however, the record failed to live up to the energy and directness of previous releases.

After leaving the Final Cut in 1990, Mills returned to his DJ roots for a while, heading back into the recording studio a year later. It was then that he joined up with Mike Banks, whom he had known from some of the early Paragon sessions (Banks had played keyboards on at least one Final Cut record). In addition to playing session guitar and generally helping out at studios like United, Banks had also been part of a Bus Boys–styled rock group called the Mechanics in the early 1980s.[19] During Mills's industrial diversion, Banks had continued to play on R&B and funk projects, as well as to produce house-inspired records with Members of the House, an early techno group that had appeared on the first *Techno!* compilation.

Mills and Banks began collaborating, spending large amounts of time behind the mixing boards. Fortunately, United Sound owner Don Davis was quite reasonable in making payment arrangements—even in the post-Motown Detroit of the early 1990s, studio time was hard to come by, and could cost anywhere from $75 to $100 per hour. "Jeff [Mills] and I understood the benefits of the technology [in the studio]," says Banks. "We'd clean [the studio] up and do sessions for free." Davis was also generous with his experience and financial advice, something musicians rarely get until it's desperately needed. Another patron, Ted Dudley, a former drummer with the soul outfit One Way, gave Mills and Banks the use of his Traxx studio in the northern suburb of Oak Park.

Just as Richie Hawtin and John Acquaviva's early attempts to impress Transmat had gone unnoticed, forcing them to start the Plus 8 label, so did Mills and Banks's plans to get the attention of Metroplex. Juan Atkins remembers the opportunity he inadvertently created for the pair: "Jeff [Mills] and Mike [Banks] came down and brought a tape, which was their first record—they wanted me to release it. But there was so much going on . . . I was flying all over the place. I didn't get to it [the record] quick enough, and they eventually dropped it themselves. I guess they have me to thank for that."

Mills and Banks's collaborations quickly grew into a concept and movement known as Underground Resistance (UR), a kind of covert musical operation set on toppling the industry establishment. Ironically, much of

UR's early output was at least as radio-friendly as that of Inner City, featuring female vocals and complete sets of lyrics. As Mills recounted to the Dutch magazine *Surreal Sound,* it would take a few releases before UR would grow into its name: "[We] thought it might be a good idea to fuse the two styles [those of Members of the House and the Final Cut] together and see what we came up with. The first track was called 'The Theory,' and then the Yolanda track came after that [both released in 1990]. We didn't really know what was happening . . . in Europe. We didn't find out what was going on until maybe the fourth release."[20]

That release turned out to be 1991's "Waveform,"[21] a record that quickly manifested UR's identity. The group made its first statement by rejecting the "white label" releases common at the time, instead releasing "Waveform" as a *black* label—perhaps an early reaction against white techno artists, spurred by Plus 8's entrance onto the scene and, more probably, the increasing influence of the European market. Apparently as early as 1991, UR had sensed that the African American component of techno music was under siege.

As different as its sound was to the Detroit techno continuum, so too was UR's image (or lack thereof). The more Mills and Banks stripped away their identity, focusing on a simple message and only the barest of details, the more notorious they became. Like the Electrifying Mojo, UR kept interviews to a minimum and let its products do the talking, with messages encoded into its song titles and even etched into the vinyl itself. This was a masterstroke, and it gave UR the upper hand when marketing to and dealing with larger labels. No one was prepared for the way Mills and Banks orchestrated their music, their band, or their business; UR's low visibility created a mystique in the minds of its fans and foes—one much larger than it could have created on its own.

Contributing to UR's mystique were militaristic tinges, drawn from both Banks's father's history in the army and the steadfast support of mentors like T. G. Williams, a three-time wounded Vietnam veteran. Williams had supported Banks's musical endeavors since 1982 and, according to Banks, was another big inspiration for the group. UR's label art, wardrobe, and rhetoric were all couched in military terms—more a token of respect than mere appropriation. Neither were the sentiments behind UR's music especially violent—foreboding would be a more appropriate description. Still, its unwavering stance against the record industry's mainstreaming of techno earned comparisons to hip-hop revolutionaries Public Enemy.

But if UR's sound was aggressive, its attitude was marked more by caution and protection of its own turf and the Detroit techno sound in general. "There's a very strong, individualistic mentality here in Detroit," said Banks in 1992. "You develop it without even noticing. I didn't notice it until I went overseas, where everyone has several real close, dear friends. Here it's like Vietnam—I'm not getting close to anybody."

The members of UR wore this attitude on their sleeves—literally. Banks is still known to wear combat boots and black or green flight jackets, adorned with U.S. Army patches and approximations of the same that incorporate the UR logo. This was also UR's garb onstage, starting with a stream of live appearances in 1992. In early UR shows, Mills and his DJ setup stood as the centerpiece, with Banks masked by a bandana and behind the keyboards on one side, Derwin Hall (aka D-Ha) on the other (also playing keyboards), and Rob Noise (aka Robert Hood or "The Vision") in front, rapping and hyping up the audience behind a stylized gas mask.

By 1991, UR's sound, image, and appearances had caught the eyes and ears of several major and independent labels, including Mute (long before it had established NovaMute for just such projects). But the closest UR came to signing with any label was its agreement to contribute the song "Elimination" to Mute's 1991 compilation *Paroxysm*. Label scouts and A&R personnel were confounded by the group's strict adherence to its underground principles. As Banks recalled at the time, some major labels simply would not recognize UR as its own label.

> We had a college kid call us from a major [label], saying, "[Are] you guys looking to get a deal?" Jeff told him, "No, we're a record label." Then the kid says [sarcastically], "I know. I know, but do you want a deal?" [Banks laughs.] A real asshole! These labels just don't understand that there's a whole generation of people out here that are tired of being prostituted by major record companies. They [the majors] are real frustrated that basement labels are placing way higher in the charts than they do.

In the process of its assault on the establishment, the European environment, and raves, UR jumped right into the fray to beat the opposition at its own game. The result was a brand of increasingly over-the-top,

IN THEIR FIRST MOTORCITY APPEARANCE...
DETROIT'S DEFENDERS OF TECHNOCRACY

UR

UNDERGROUND
RESISTANCE

SUNDAY SEPT 6 - STATE THEATRE
2115 WOODWARD • DETROIT • 961-5450
DOORS OPEN 9PM, 18 & OVER, $10
THIS PERFORMANCE IS PART OF THE "PANIC STRIKES AGAIN" PARTY

PARTY FLYERS AS HARBINGERS OF
DOOM? IN ITS MOST INTENSE PERIOD,
UNDERGROUND RESISTANCE BRINGS ITS
BRAND OF "PUNISHMENT" TO A LIVE
AUDIENCE ON SEPTEMBER 8, 1992.
(Gary Arnett)

experimental, and anthem-like techno. Ironically, the European crowds reveled in it; whatever havoc UR wreaked on their synapses, they kept wanting more.

As a testament to this process, UR created the 1991 single "The Punisher," named after the ruthless vigilante from Marvel Comics. Like Cybersonik, UR had begun stretching the limits of what was funky, supplanting melody with simplistic, abrasive riffs. But UR never quite gave in all the way, usually backing its aggressive sounds with round after round of high-caliber frequencies—exactly the kind of punishment the European crowd had been asking for. Not only was "The Punisher" one of UR's biggest underground hits, but after its release, the group's logo began to look very much like that of the comic book character, with the letters "UR" replacing the teeth in the stylized "death's head" design.

After UR took its tour to European audiences in 1991 and saw how enthusiastically its blend of talent and antagonism was received, the group expanded the scope of its subversive approach. Some describe the UR mystique as "mythology," suggesting that all of its stances and mandates were part of a larger *anti-marketing* marketing scheme, and should therefore be questioned. But the term also implies that somewhere, someone believed in what was going on—and in places like Manchester, Belgium, and the Hague, UR found its kindred spirits.

As a tribute to the strong European underground ethic discovered on the tour (which must have caught UR by surprise to some degree), the label released a series known as World Power Alliance (WPA) in 1992.[22] Starting with these records, UR showed development far beyond its simple, anonymous beginnings. The group and its associates had grown into a wonderfully complex and vivid array of images and theories. This was the stage, if any, when UR rose to the level of myth, during a period of expansion and even deeper experimentation.

Logical Progression

UR also found itself within a larger context at home, as part of the collective known as Submerge, formed in 1991. Submerge was essentially a new business model and standard for the Detroit techno underground. The idea was simple: gather the best talent—musical, clerical, financial, and so on—and form a collaborate environment that could survive independently of major labels. Christa Weatherspoon was one of the first "non-artists" to come aboard.

> I was aboard before Submerge formed legally, helping out some of the labels and finding out what they were having problems doing. I have a degree in corporate finance, so it's not like I have any plans to make music, [but] I definitely enjoy the business side of Submerge. One of things that I could see early on was that it would practically put labels out of business [to] not only create the music but [also] handle the day-to-day administration.

By bringing like-minded people of various talents together in a collaborative environment, Submerge revolutionized the underground, making it a viable economic community unto itself and allowing artists to retain their artistic independence. Supported by this solid foundation, the labels under Submerge guidance had room to experiment.

Two of the first projects nurtured under the Submerge umbrella were UR conceptual side projects—X-101 and X-102. An X-101 EP went on to launch the German label Tresor in 1991, which also released X-102's legendary 1992 album *X-102 Discovers the Rings of Saturn*. *Saturn* was no ordinary concept album, at least not by the same prog-rock standards the term implies. The album featured fourteen songs, each named after the planet's rings and moons, with track lengths (and subsequently track *widths* on the vinyl copies) corresponding to the actual sizes of and distances between the celestial bodies.

The heavens were also the inspiration behind Detroit's Red Planet label,[23] a Submerge member and focused outlet for the jazz influence in techno. In addition to being a challenge to express (given the improvisational nature of jazz and the programmed nature of techno), this jazz influence had been suppressed during techno's more aggressive streak in 1990–91. Red Planet allowed techno a return to its more personal and emotive beginnings and leanings, as did the music of a series of UR-related groups that included Mike Banks: Nation 2 Nation, World 2 World, and Galaxy 2 Galaxy. The latter, a solo production of Banks's, recorded some of the most spiritual sounds ever committed to vinyl in Detroit, including moving tributes to Geronimo on "Astral Apache" and to Bruce and Brandon Lee on "Journey of the Dragons."[24]

Coinciding with the advent of *Global Techno Power (GTP)*, a fanzine started in 1992 by Robert Hood, visuals also became increasingly important. *GTP* shared space and resources with Submerge and helped connect Detroit to the emerging techno and rave scenes worldwide. Centered around *GTP*, the dozen or so labels swapped ideas and took on bizarre, tongue-in-cheek artist names like Life after Mutation and Dr. Kevorkian. In a way, the creativity buzzing around the Submerge offices was not unlike that of Techno Boulevard in the mid- to late 1980s.

As Detroit's underground community widened in the early 1990s, combativeness between the local labels shifted as they realized how wide the competitive ring was. Truth be told, Underground Resistance would need to save its energy for some very real messages it traded with the majors in 2000. UR's DJ Rolando had a runaway hit in the song "Jaguar," and, unable to license it from them, Sony Records Germany commissioned a "note-for-note" cover version. UR and its representatives traded numerous e-mails trying to get Sony to back off, but Sony in turn licensed their cover to BMG and things got even more complicated. Ultimately, it was the original Underground Resistance spirit that prevailed, and they fought fire with fire, releasing a special edition of the original on sister label 430 West with exclusive remixes in an attempt to beat the majors at their own game.

Explains Hawtin, "Everyone had that kind of mentality and philosophy about going against the industry. We were all fighting the battle of distribution and getting things out there." Adds Banks, "In retrospect, those were some great times with Plus 8. In fact, we still laugh about [those days] now. Unfortunately, no one has stepped up into the ring quite like Plus 8 used to. We await our next challenger, because for us it's a forever war and not a war for fame, fortune, or females — it's a war for soul that started long before UR. We are an electronic continuation of it."

Insistent Rhythm

Just when it seemed that techno's next wave of stabilization would settle around a second triumvirate (Plus 8, UR, and Retroactive), its ranks began to grow exponentially. Several other labels would materialize by the end of 1991, but one in particular, formed by members of the techno group Octave One, served as a sort of gateway for them all.

The odd men out on the *Techno 2* compilation were Octave One, a group comprising Lawrence, Lenny, and Lynell Burden — the eldest three of five brothers. The Burdens had been recording their own music for years before their introduction to techno in the late 1980s, first exploring industrial, new wave, and jazz sounds. Slightly more practiced than your average self-starting knob-twiddlers, Octave One may have figured it had an edge and would easily become a project on one of the three "big" Detroit techno sources (Metroplex, KMS, and Transmat). Instead, it encountered a lack of attention, and even apprehension, as it lay outside the original clique of artists who had collaborated down on Detroit's Techno Boulevard. As Damon Booker suggests, the first techno compilation was "like the closing of the loop. After the album it was like 'Who is that?'"

Still, Octave One managed to find a way onto the second compilation, courtesy of its only "in" — Detroit techno producer Anthony "Shake" Shakir. As Lawrence Burden recalls, "We met Shake through Terrell Langston, a mutual friend. He [Langston] was doing hip-hop with Shake back then.[25]

He used to hear our stuff and he thought it was techno, so he thought we should hook up with Shake. We kinda picked up his vibe a little bit and our sound got smoothed out. The funny thing is that we used to do full songs, and once we got with Shake we started doing tracks!"

Shakir essentially produced Octave One's passport into the scene: the surprise 1990 hit "I Believe." Featuring dreamy, soft-spoken vocals by friend Lisa Newberry and melancholy, Detroit-style chords, "I Believe" became a techno spiritual of sorts, on a par with much of May's material and English group 808 State's "Pacific State." Says Lawrence Burden, "At the time, they were compiling the second *Techno!* album and all of the tracks were selected. Shake sent 'I Believe' to them 'cause he was sending the masters for one of the songs from the Transmat camp. They ended up bumping somebody off the album and put our song on [instead]."

The brothers won't divulge whose song they replaced, but they do recall that while their song failed to impress May, it was validated by Neil Rushton, who immediately sniffed out another hit. And though the marketing push was behind Area 10's "Love Take Me Over," Lenny Burden recalls all the attention paid to "I Believe": "'Love Take Me Over' was supposed to be the next 'Big Fun.' It ["Love Take Me Over"] was [the first song on side A] and we were [the first song on side B] — both on the outer bands [of the vinyl]. It was a complete surprise to everyone. You have to realize that no one really knew us. We had just gone in to rent some studio time — the only person who really knew us was Shake. We paid no dues."

Despite the success of "I Believe" (there was even talk of putting the group on the English TV show *Top of the Pops*), Octave One was kept out of the loop, shielded from the buzz it had generated. But after continually hearing about the song's success secondhand, the brothers eventually realized that their sound was valuable enough to keep producing. They stopped working out of Lenny's apartment, now overgrown with patch cords and MIDI cables, and moved their operations to 430 West Eight Mile Road. Taking its name directly from the address, the brothers' new 430 West label quickly became (literally and figuratively) a haven for artists who hadn't yet started their own labels. Jay Denham, Eddie Fowlkes, and budding Detroit house producer Terrence Parker all got boosts from the new label in the early to mid-1990s.

One new label that emerged in part as a result of help from 430 West was Seventh City, formed in 1993 by Daniel Bell, whose material and interests had become increasingly divergent from those of Plus 8 and Probe. Helping Bell start up the label was Claude Young, a quick-learning DJ who is now one of the few such talents to be compared to Mills in terms of technique. The Seventh City label released only a handful of records, but Bell later reclaimed the name to start his own distribution business and eventually resurrected the label on his own in 1995.

The Groove That Won't Stop

In general, the Detroit techno community was becoming increasingly more fluid and nonlinear as the mid-1990s approached, shaking up and widening its definition and niche. In some cases, this niche expanded to include artists outside Detroit. In Brooklyn, New York, for example, an enormous amount of talent seemed to pour out of the city all at once. Centered on their Brooklyn record store Groove (now Sonic Groove in Manhattan), brothers Frankie and Adam Mitchell—professionally known as DJs Frankie Bones and Adam X—began holding events they called Storm Rave. Adam's girlfriend, Heather Heart, who also worked at Groove, disseminated event highlights, information, and manifestos via the collective's fanzine, *Under One Sky.* By 1992, Brooklyn's small, spur-of-the-moment happenings had snowballed into in extended scene that included seminal New York artists like Joey Beltram and Mundo Muzique (who, together as Second Phase, recorded the rave anthem "Mentasm" in 1991).

While Brooklyn's new collective was blowing up, one of techno's earliest and biggest personalities was emerging just across the bridge in Manhattan. Behind the pseudonyms Voodoo Child, Brainstorm, Barracuda, UHF, and Moby was Connecticut-born Richard Melville Hall.[26] While recording for New York's independent Instinct label, Hall got noticed for his kinetic dance tracks and early experimentation with ambient techno, evident on tracks such as "Mobility," released in November 1990. "Mobility" cemented Hall's use of "Moby" as his artist name, but it was the B-side that promoted him to the world of pop culture. "Go" was built on the sinister strings of "Laura's Theme," from the *Twin Peaks* soundtrack, and a sampled call-to-action from Tones on Tail's song of the same name. "Go" was a huge sensation, reaching No. 10 on the U.K. Gallup Top 40 in November 1991 and helping land Hall deals with Mute and Elektra Records. From this point on, however, Hall's personality seemed to eclipse his music, with the media latching onto facets such as his devout Christianity and veganism. At first, it seemed gimmicks and novelties directed attention to his music, such as his single "Thousand" —a song that clocks in at 1,000 bpm and made the *Guinness Book of World Records*—and a funked-up reworking of the "James Bond Theme" for the 1997 film *Tomorrow Never Dies*. Ultimately, his consistency, longevity, business acumen (such as licensing every track off his 1999 album *Play,* which sold no less than ten million copies), and charity work have earned him a quite a bit more respect.

Urbane Contemporary

While the underground was home to much of techno's development in the United States at this time, there were also some surprisingly creative developments "above ground," as groups like Inner City continued to negotiate relationships with the mainstream industry.

Perhaps feeling the need to atone for its second album (the failed R&B crossover *Fire* in 1990), Inner City found new energy by heading back to the basics. Saunderson and Grey both knew that soul music was built on gospel and that therefore techno and house music still carried with them a strong sense of spirituality. On their third album, *Praise,* released in 1992, the two wrote songs like "Let It Reign" and "Hallelujah," with Grey reaching back to her early days of singing in church. The masterstroke was combining these triumphant sounds with that of English group Altern 8 (Chris Peat and Mark Archer, also known as Nexus 21). The result merged classic Detroit techno hymns with Altern 8's piano/breakbeat sound to form one of the most unique collaborations in techno to date. Other Detroit artists would also find ways to incorporate spiritual themes, including Model 500's 1993 record "I See the Light"; Richie Hawtin's "Spiritual High," released in 1992–93 under the pseudonym Up!; and Octave One's "I Believe."

Chicago's Li'l Louis (born Louis Sims, son of Chess blues drummer Robert "Bobby" Sims) would also break with form, as one of the few house artists at the time to aggressively pursue an album-based career. Riding the wave of his international success and platinum twelve-inch single "French Kiss" in 1989, Louis landed a record deal with Epic. His next album, *From the Mind of Li'l Louis* (released that same year), was followed by *Journey with the Lonely* in 1992, helping to break ground for African American house and techno artists in dealing with major labels. Unfortunately, Louis's precedent is more often overlooked than given proper credit.

Origins of a Sound

Because most of Detroit's techno scene went back underground in the early 1990s, it required an efficient and affordable means of recording music. Vinyl was still the medium of choice, so Detroit reconnected with the remnants of its old record industry. Local businesses like Archer Record Pressing Plant and National Sound became critical in providing techno artists with the expediency and technical finesse needed to compete in a global market.

The Archer Record Pressing Plant, located in Detroit, is the last remaining business of its kind in Michigan, started in 1964 by Norm Archer. Though these days it's looked after by Norm's grandson, Mike, in the "lean years" of the 1980s, Joe Archer (Norm's son) ran the company. "We were contemplating the demise of vinyl. Everybody said vinyl was history," says Joe. "But we kept the doors open." In fact, just as the plant went fully automatic, Detroit's techno labels grew from the initial three to a few dozen and business at the plant began to pick up. This helped Archer outlast the mainstream's jump to CDs.

On the other side of town, demand kept another link to Motown busy behind wood paneling and matte black interfaces. The late Ron Murphy headed up Sound Enterprises, a mastering lab in Wayne, Michigan, that catered to the techno client. Mastering is the all-important staging area between art and industry, when electrical impulses are turned into vibrations and etched into lacquer.

It takes a special ear to prepare a recording for this process, the kind Murphy started honing at age twelve. "I'd just play records for hours," he said. "In 1959 I bought my first record—Marv Johnson's 'Come to Me.'" This was the beginning of the world's largest Motown collection, earning Murphy the nickname "Motown Murphy." Strangely enough, Murphy's first experience cutting records can also be traced back to this era: "I saw an ad on the back of a comic book that read '$9.99—Record Your Voice at Home!'" After hearing the disappointingly tinny playback on cardboard records, Murphy said, "This isn't going to do it for me."

Murphy would eventually upgrade to better equipment, learning recording nuances from some of the old studio hands at Special Recordings, one of the many smaller studios that handled spillover business during the Motown era. After the last of these studios shut down, Murphy opened National Sound Corporation (later renamed Sound Enterprises) in 1989, buying and selling used records.[27] Although it was simply a way to keep enjoying music (Murphy had since moved into selling insurance), National soon became a catalyst for Detroit's early techno pioneers. "What happened was that Derrick May and Juan Atkins came in, probably looking for old records," Murphy recalls. "They didn't know that we had been cutting dubs with this old lathe we had in the back."

After stunning May and Atkins with a rich, bass-heavy dub, Murphy started cutting records regularly, eventually cutting over a thousand "sides" a year. He also added some old flourishes like inscribing messages into the run-out grooves and cutting a record backward so that it plays from the inside out. One of Murphy's own innovations was the "locked groove," a closed loop on a record that plays indefinitely—one of the greatest tools a DJ could ask for. As Murphy recalled, it was a happy accident.

> I had been noticing that a lot of [techno] was very repetitive—I couldn't help but notice! I kept thinking about that. Jeff Mills came in and said, "I got a thing here called 'The Rings of Saturn.' What can we do different?" I said, "All your stuff is these loops, right? I wonder if I can loop it on a record in one turn—like a ring." He started writing out the information for his labels like a lot of them would while I was working, and I happened to do it. I didn't realize that it had to be 133 1/3 bpm for it to work at the time, but his track was 133 1/3 bpm just by accident! I played the loop and Jeff looked up 'cause he noticed that something was supposed to change. It was perfect. "That's the loop I was telling you about," I said. He jumped up and said, "Do you know what this means?!"

Murphy also grew to understand the dynamics of techno, learning along with its early producers. Though techno has particular quirks that require special attention, the basic sound was similar to what Murphy already knew inside and out. "I wasn't interested in cutting 'country & western' music," Murphy explained. "When I grew up in the studio, it was all R&B and soul with the heavy low end. To a certain degree, techno is the same thing. That's how I put together the system. I was kind of lucky that being in Detroit gave the business a boost. In a way, it works both ways, because these guys come in and are able to pretty much get the sound that they want."

This sound—the minute difference in the way its records are mastered —may be part of the Detroit techno mystique. While most of Murphy's trade secrets were kept close to the vest, he explained that the difference mostly comes from the uniqueness and antiquity of the equipment. "The sound is a little different because I use a system that nobody else in the world uses," he said. "Maybe there are some in South America, but basically I'm the only one cutting so that it's tuned a certain way. Also, the amp blew early on so we made our own amp modules, which changed the sound." Murphy was also responsible for encouraging the propaganda-style messages of Plus 8 and UR, suggesting that they be inscribed right into the run-out grooves of their records. Many hours were spent in the National Sound office, contemplating exactly how these "words of wisdom" should read.

Although some of today's record labels master and press their records elsewhere, there are only about a dozen places left in the entire country that provide either service. This fragile section of the music industry was invaluable to techno and once attracted as much interest as the music itself. A Japanese music fanzine once interviewed Murphy, trying to quantify "the Detroit sound" and requesting close-up snapshots of his hands. "They were quite extensive," Murphy recalled.

Both Archer and Sound Enterprises benefited from techno's widening popularity for many years. But ask any of Detroit's artists and producers and they'll tell it the other way around. "We needed them," says Lenny Burden of Octave One. "With Ron [Murphy], you could actually be part of the process—he taught people how to engineer their own records. The same goes for Archer. Being able to see your records being pressed . . . it's almost a spiritual thing."

6

Applied Technology

The Myth of Techno
Collides with Reality,
1991–2001

WE ONLY DID A HANDFUL OF GIGS AS "THE KNOB-TWIDDLERS" AND
THEN ALL OF A SUDDEN WE ASSUMED JOHN, PAUL, GEORGE, AND
RINGO [STATUS] ONSTAGE. WE TOOK IT TO AMERICA—AND
AMERICANS MAKE YOU WORK LIKE FUCK, DON'T THEY? THEY STAND
THERE AND THEY GO "ENTERTAIN ME!"
DARREN PARTINGTON (808 STATE)

I DON'T FEEL ANY KINSHIP STYLISTICALLY OR BUSINESS-WISE
WITH THE "ELECTRONICA" BOOM, DESPITE THE FACT THAT,
WITHOUT IT, I'M NOT SURE WE WOULD EXIST.
SAM VALENTI IV, OWNER AND A&R, *GHOSTLY INTERNATIONAL*

In the early 1990s, the rave scene dramatically heightened techno's profile, exposing it to mass audiences in Europe and, later, the United States. In Detroit, artists responded by heading back underground, choosing to avoid mainstream co-optation and compromises with major labels. At the same time, increasing numbers of multinational artists came to the forefront outside the United States, bred in a culture much more saturated with raves and the sounds of techno. Surprisingly, many of these artists met with success as they crisscrossed the globe and "crossed over" into pop.

Band Width

For some European musicians, assimilation into the established industry came with seemingly little effort. One of these was Manchester's 808 State, a group that managed to integrate the lengthened time frames and repetitive structures of dance music with the framework and energy of live rock 'n' roll.

808 State was formed in 1988 by Graham Massey (an ex-funk player with the band Biting Tongues), Gerald Simpson, and Martin Price, owner of Manchester's Eastern Bloc record shop. It was at Price's record shop that Massey and Simpson had started recording as the Hit Squad, one of the many British hip-hop crews embracing acid house at the time. Eventually, Massey and Simpson started taking conceptual cues from Price, and the three began collaborating as 808 State.

808 State's intense *Newbuild* EP, released in 1988, was next-generation English acid house, more direct and far more sinister than the sounds coming from Baby Ford and S'Express down in London. After a falling-out concerning payment for his work on the album (and 808's subsequent success with "Pacific State," a song he cowrote), Simpson left 808 State in 1989 to set out on his own. Massey filled the empty slot by enlisting Darren Partington and Andy Barker, previously of another Manchester hip-hop crew called the Spinmasters.

Now that they were a four-piece outfit (Massey, Price, Partington, and Barker), 808 State began to grow in a very band-like way.[1] Says Partington, "Basically we're a production team that appears to be a band onstage. We're not an image-based band; we change all the time—a record label's nightmare." Still, once "Pacific State" had been released on the 1989 *Quadrastate* EP, 808 State knew that its path would not be of the "faceless techno producer" ilk.

The American hip-hop label Tommy Boy showed its keen ears and long-range thinking by signing 808 State in 1990, early in the group's career. According to Steve Knutson, a Tommy Boy executive who helped bring the group to the United States, "At the time that those records came out, the word 'techno' really wasn't even used [in the United States]. 808 State was looked [on] as more of an alternative/dance type of group." This put

GRAHAM MASSEY (*LEFT*), DARREN PARTINGTON (*MIDDLE*), AND ANDY BARKER (*RIGHT*) OF 808 STATE, LOOKING EVERY BIT AS ARTY AND ENERGIZED AS THEIR MUSIC. (Phil Knott)

808 State in an entirely different context than it had been in Europe, where it had been framed as an extension of Manchester's rave and techno scene. Instead, Tommy Boy placed 808 State next to more guitar-oriented groups onstage and in record bins, separating the group from both the Detroit and U.K. techno scenes that had inspired it—not that this detracted from the group's excitement about being signed to the label. Says Partington, "When we got to America, like about 1989, we were on Tommy Boy. We [had] collected Tommy Boy as DJs—they pioneered a specific sound. People still feel that passionate about the label—and we were signed to it!"

Though 808 State was named after the quintessential hip-hop drum machine—the Roland TR-808—the group made no attempt to disguise its techno roots. There were even strains of Cybotron's "Techno City" woven into the fabric of "Donkey Doctor" on its first proper album, 1989's *808:90.*[2] These references became less and less obvious, however, as the group's productions became more and more ornate. 808 State was determined to grow into the alternative market and its role as a techno "band," though there wasn't really any precedent as such. And like many other techno producers of the early 1990s, 808 State would run into puzzled audiences and critics alike as it pushed the boundaries of what a techno album should be.

The group's second offering, 1991's *Ex:El,* was even more ambitious, jumping from whirling, elaborate vignettes like "Nephatiti," to modern mood-pop featuring Bernard Sumner of New Order ("Spanish Heart") and Icelandic singer-songwriter Björk Gudmundsdóttir ("Ooops"). "At the time, Björk was in the Sugarcubes," says Partington. "She was the queen of indie. . . . Back to the purists [who would say], 'You don't do that, you don't bring people like her in here with us!'" Given Björk's strong subsequent support of techno, it's clear that 808 State had a knack for finding vocalists and musicians to complement the genre. "[It was just] forward thinking," says Partington. "If you try to force people to buy it [techno]— you have to invent this whole [new] subculture to go with it."

Another European band that assimilated surprisingly easily into the mainstream was England's LFO,[3] also signed to Tommy Boy in 1990. LFO had helped define the Sheffield "bleep and bass" era with a much simpler and less ornate sound than that of 808 State. When it came to marketing LFO, Tommy Boy's emphasis was placed purely on the sounds of the group's recordings—specifically its namesake low-frequency bass vibrations, evident on the rumbling 1990 single "LFO" and 1991's "We Are Back." Tommy Boy even went as far as placing semi-serious stickers on LFO's album labels and packaging, stating, "BEWARE OF BASS. Warning: Tommy Boy Music, Inc., its affiliates, and licensees disclaim any and all liability for speaker damage resulting from the playback of this sound recording." As Knutson recalls: "We [Tommy Boy] didn't even promote or market [LFO] to the more alternative type of dance audience. What we did was market it more to the Miami Bass [a grittier, sometimes salacious variant of electro] and the southern audience that was still really sympathetic to the sounds of [Afrika Bambaataa's] 'Planet Rock.' And, even though it was mostly instrumental stuff, we ended up selling over thirty thousand LFO albums."

N-joi—also from England—was signed by RCA Records in 1991 and helped write the script for crossover success in the United States, especially with their sampled rallying cries of "Let the bass kick" and "Drop the bass now!" (both from N-joi's 1991 EP *Mindflux*). As one of the first groups to combine techno compositions with a wealth of sampled breakbeats, N-joi found itself in the techno/hip-hop fringe that grew into what became known as hard core. The group's exposure in the United States, however, was limited to only one EP—almost miniscule when compared with other crossover acts, such as the Prodigy.

The Prodigy's founder, Liam Howlett, like so many other English techno and acid house fans of the early 1990s, was grounded in the fundamentals of hip-hop. As a former "brit-hop" DJ himself, it was natural that Howlett would begin joining the breakbeat to up-tempo house music in his own compositions. *What Evil Lurks,* released in 1990, got the group's trio (Howlett, Leeroy Thornhill, and dancer Keith Flint) signed to XL Records, a U.K. label. The Prodigy's second single, "Charly," was its watershed moment, codifying its breakbeat approach and scoring a No. 1 hit on the U.K. National Dance Chart and a No. 3 slot on the U.K. Gallup Top 40 in 1991. But success came at a small price—ravers initially judged the scattershot rhythms of "breakbeat house" (and the many juvenile "Charly" clones) as anathema to the steady four-count bliss they had enjoyed since 1988's "Summer of Love." The U.K. dance music magazine *Mixmag* even went as far as asking the following on a 1992 cover: "Did 'Charly' Kill Rave?"

This division between ravers and breakbeat fans would eventually widen to become a stumbling block for many other groups as the fledgling breakbeat sound evolved into modern jungle and drum & bass. The Prodigy, however, managed to stay above the fray, riding its new image as dance music outlaws to continued success in the United Kingdom. It was no small accident that the group finally broke through to U.S. audiences when it donned punk-era trappings and promoted Flint from dancer to vocalist/front man. Aside from brief commitments early on, however, U.S. record labels didn't know quite what to do with the Prodigy —until Madonna gave it the outlet it needed on her Maverick label in 1997. The rest is recent "electronica" history: the group's 1997 album *The Fat of the Land,* which featured the monster hit singles "Firestarter" and "Breathe," quickly went platinum, selling more than two million copies in less than two years. However far removed the Prodigy may be from a definition of "techno," the group is surely one of electronic dance music's biggest success stories.

However, between 1993 and 1997 the rave scene found prolonged success in its expansion on the European continent, leaving the United Kingdom in the lurch. While many U.K. labels were forced to fold, at least one survived—thanks in part to its dedicated A&R efforts. Sheffield's Warp Records had begun redefining itself in 1993, when it began releasing records in what it called the *Artificial Intelligence* series. With this series, Warp hoped to comment on the concept of music as artificial life—from something as simple as a computer virus or "bot" to the larger concept that techno has a life of its own and perhaps an agenda larger than our own.

The *Artificial Intelligence* series started with a compilation by the same name, introducing new audiences to the work of Aphex Twin, Autechre, Black Dog Productions, B12, Richie Hawtin, Speedy J, and the Orb. Several of these artists had taken inspiration from the melodic wing of Detroit techno and the recordings of Derrick May and Carl Craig. For a lot of listeners, particularly those who had lost the taste or stamina for hard-core techno parties, the *Artificial Intelligence* records were a perfect antidote.

By about 1994 — not long after the release of the series — the phrase "artificial intelligence" had become a generic term, used to represent a more sophisticated rejection of the rave scene. Variants of the term were "intelligent techno" and "intelligent dance music," both of which originally carried the same sentiments as "artificial intelligence" but evolved into a kind of elitist badge of honor for those who enjoyed electronic dance music but weren't keen on the more populist aspects of its culture.

Despite this negative etymological trend, however, the *Artificial Intelligence* series broke through to U.S. audiences, helping them start to come to grips with techno. Licensed to the American TVT label (original home of Nine Inch Nails and current owner of Wax Trax records), most of the series was introduced to the American public in 1993 and 1994. By this time, the U.S. industry and press had had more time to think about ways to present and market this vein of techno, and despite poor sales (reportedly less than five thousand copies per release), *Artificial Intelligence* received a significant amount of press coverage. "Everybody talks about those records and how they were the first techno records they heard," says TVT's director of A&R Adam Shore. "They didn't sell that well, but at least they were out there. The Detroit techno CDs weren't out there, the Chicago house CDs weren't out there, but these were."

Trans-Europe Express

Though not quite as many bands were exported with the same success as U.K. counterparts, pockets of Germany's electronic music scene began to change. What some fans in America would recognize as "industrial" music morphed into an electronic dance music scene that today could be considered the functional capital of techno.

Following a huge peak, Kraftwerk's influence on rock — Bowie's "Berlin" trilogy of albums — another sound known as "techno," or sometimes "tekno," emerged in Frankfurt, largely credited to Talla 2XLC (Andreas

Tomalla). "Talla" is a prolific artist who also ran the Zoth Ommog label, founded the "Technoclub" in the Dorian Gray, and kicked off the German techno magazine *Frontpage*. He was also a member of the group Moskwa TV, who released a single called "Tekno Talk" in 1985. Unlike Detroit techno, however, this "tekno" was more connected to "hi-NRG" and "electronic body music (EBM)"—styles that were strictly European.

As Europe began redefining itself in 1989 and 1990, its youth constructed a new underground dance music scene, with Detroit techno serving as a chief influence. In England, the rave scene was at its peak, helping the English erase their inhibited past one ecstatic night at a time. In Germany, there were larger reasons to celebrate. The collapse of the Berlin Wall in November 1989 gave techno "Renaissance man" Dimitri Hegemann and his cohorts on the Interfisch label a window of opportunity, one that was larger and more literal than that which Detroit's youth had taken advantage of in the early 1980s.

The area around the wall that had traditionally separated East from West still existed as a sort of "no-man's-land," and the buildings in the area remained largely unoccupied through the nearly year-long reunification process. By 1991, however, Potsdamer Platz had a new resident: Hegemann and Co. While searching for a new club location, the former Interfisch crew had stumbled on a series of underground rooms with iron bars, which had once served as vaults for the now-defunct Wertheim department store (once the largest store in Europe). The group's new club became known as Tresor, a German word meaning "vault" or "safe." It was an unlikely but incredible place to start. Recalls Hegemann, "We were the place where East and West kids came together, musically. We found our style—it was definitely oriented toward minimal Detroit sounds, and then after a year and half we had our own crowd."

Tresor brought new life to the careers of many Detroit artists. Santonio Echols, Eddie Fowlkes, and Blake Baxter were among the club's first bookings, alongside established Berlin DJs such as Dr. Motte and Tanith. Tresor, the label, was also built on a few dozen releases from Detroit, starting with the 1991 X-101 project from Underground Resistance.

Hegemann was intent on building a connection between Berlin and Detroit, as evidenced from the 1993 compilation *Tresor II: Berlin-Detroit: A Techno Alliance,* made available to U.S. audiences through NovaMute. There were even plans to open a Tresor club in Detroit, which eventually fizzled out. Says Hegemann, "Musically, we had this help from Detroit, and after a while we thought we'd give something back. I thought it was a good challenge. There are so many possibilities [in Detroit] and I thought something could be done. Why is Detroit still asleep?"

By the mid-1990s, Germany was close to defining its own style of techno, as the Detroit, Frankfurt, and Berlin definitions began bleeding into one another. Still, the controversy over the style's ancestry—whether it stemmed from "tekno" or Detroit's "techno"—periodically reared its ugly head. As Tresor's booking agent, Alexandra Dröner, explains, "That [spelling with a *k*] was kind of a joke—to show with a word the hard-core quality [of German techno]. For us it was a joke: 'Yeah, he played tekno with four *k*s!' Years later, I became very militant [about techno's Detroit origins] and so I began to [pronounce it with the English *ch* and] say 'tesshno' again."

The crew at Hard Wax Records, another hub of Berlin's techno scene, wasn't exactly militant about the music's origins, but they held the principles of Detroit techno in high regard—especially those communicated to the store via the music (and faxed manifestos) of Underground Resistance. Started in 1989 as a no-frills record store in Berlin's Kreuzberg district, Hard Wax is probably best known for being at the center of one of Berlin's most interesting techno movements: the legendary group Basic Channel. Started by store owner Mark Ernestus and Moritz von Oswald, originally a percussionist and later part of the Tresor camp, the group's reputation stemmed from its ability to hide in plain sight, never being quoted or photographed yet remaining very much in the spotlight from 1993 to 1994.

Basic Channel's music was a near-total reconstruction of techno and house: starting from the principles of Jamaican "dub" and working back to the four-count beat conducive to club play. Records like "Phylyps Trak," "Quadrant Dub," and "Octagon" (all released in 1994) incorporate basslines that sound like pond ripples and beats buried under a mile of gauze—even the ultra-distressed typography of the label art reflects a murky composition. Basic Channel's ideas would go on to inspire the work of Vainquer, Porter Ricks, Monolake, and a host of other innovative German techno artists.

Germany's growing scene in the early 1990s was the beginning of techno's decentralization. From this point on, one could never predict where the next influential label or artist would emerge. Ironically, as much as it spread from country to country, techno began to create its second logical center in Berlin (after Detroit). Berlin has also swiftly become Germany's music capital. Starting with Hegemann's efforts, the rise of German hip-hop, the move of Universal Music from Hamburg in 2002 and many artists streaming into the city from other countries—you can begin to understand its rise to cultural prominence.

Follow the Beat

Although not necessarily chronologically "next," two countries whose scenes grew organically and most rapidly were Belgium and the Netherlands. The latter did so almost from scratch, without the same kind of precedents for "techno." For the first half of the 1990s, new Dutch techno artists such as Terrace (Stefan Robbers) emphasized beauty through technology, mirroring Detroit's most melodic output. This would stand in stark contrast to the faster, noisier sound of "Gabber" that followed soon after.

One antidote to that apocalyptic trend was Marsel Van Der Wielen's Delsin label, founded in 1996. Initially an outlet for his own work (under the Peel Seamus alias), Delsin took many ingredients of Detroit techno—strong emotional contrasts, star-sailing chords, and so forth—and built a roster of artists more or less around this aesthetic.

Another way Van Der Wielen set his label apart was in the visual communication on his record art and Web presence. Early on nearly everything had a black-and-white treatment, blending in mystery and cheeky, sci-fi naïveté—sort of like a self-effacing version of Underground Resistance's early twelve-inch singles. Hearing Van Der Wielen explain his specific Detroit influences, one can see how he might have divined this approach.

> I grew up with [Carl Craig's] Retroactive and Planet E from their very beginning. They were really a landmark for me. Both the wide approach [to the music] as the elusive artwork which came with many EPs. The 69 and the Piece releases, for example, were and are so far from what you would call a *blueprint* of Detroit techno. They were all about creativity. Also how [Jeff Mills's] Axis was run, [where] each EP seemed a tight strong concept in combination with the artwork . . . gave that label a very strong image and appeal.

Delsin, like Plus 8, was also global very early on. In fact, for a Dutch label supposedly taking cues from Detroit, it odd to see that Van Der

Wielen released records from only two Detroit artists, and only a half dozen or so from the Netherlands. Delsin never went out of its way to fulfill the Detroit legacy, and perhaps that is why so many found the label to be so authentic. Still it is an odd thing to be considered a standard bearer for a genre when its home base is still actively producing music.

The Belgian influence on techno was far less gradual, adopting and adapting the Detroit sound about as quickly as England in roughly the same time period. What gave it source material and continuity was the growing Ghent-based label R&S Records (named for owners Renaat Vandepapeliere and Sabine Maes), a steady source of energetic techno for the rest of Europe. R&S moved away from Belgium's focus on new beat, releasing dozens of influential techno records in only a few years. These included the R-Tyme project in 1989, featuring Derrick May and D-Wynn; the classic single "House of God" by Chicago's DHS in 1991; and two groundbreaking EPs from Aphex Twin in 1992.

The Elypsia label entered the mix in 1996, a Brussels-based label that released several albums from Detroit artists, including Dark Comedy (Kenny Larkin), Fade to Black (Jay Denham), and Scan 7. Charleroi artist Fabrice Lig (real name: Fabrice Ligny) recorded for the label during this time frame under the name "Bug Orchestra." Lig was inspired by Detroit early on, hearing Inner City's "Big Fun," but would become connected to its scene several years later with his remix "Banjo" by E-Dancer—yet another Kevin Saunderson alias. "Belgium is the kingdom of Hard Techno," he proclaims. "And I don't have any place on this scene . . . in other countries you have some other place where you can find other kinds of electronic music. It was really rare in Belgium."[4]

In contrast to Lig's account, the nascent European techno scene in the early 1990s was a bit more open and dynamic. Together with the Netherlands, the United Kingdom, and Germany, Belgium completed the central structure of European support and enthusiasm. "By 1990–91, things became more interesting," says Neil Rushton. "Instead of three people in Detroit, you suddenly had twenty-three people making techno, in Belgium, in Sheffield."[5]

In varying ways, these countries held a torch for Detroit—not just its techno music but the *concept* of the city that was encoded in so much vinyl. Ideas set in motion by Juan Atkins and Cybotron, promoters pumping life into historic sites and forgotten spaces, and, of course, actual record label headquarters and artist dwellings. This love for the city was but one aspect discussed on 313, the Detroit Techno Mailing List.[6] It was there that fans from these countries and dozens of others learned, shared, and obsessed over Detroit and its music.

Like all long-distance love affairs, there *has* to be a moment where the need for intimacy overwhelms. For Detroit, this meant that the techno "massive," as it were, began to visit. Yes, the capital of the post-industrial Midwest was becoming a vacation destination—for *young people.* 313 was an early facilitator, as many music mailing lists with similar early 1990s histories were functional extensions of the rave community. Whereas most are very local in scope, such as sf-raves, mw-raves, and ne-raves (San Francisco, Midwest, and Northeast respectively), 313's reach is global. Bits finally gave way to atoms in December 1999, where a party by and for 313 list members was held in the Detroit suburb of Redford. In attendance were several international visitors, including Otto Koppius, Hans Veneman, Wibo Lammerts, and Klaas-Jan Jongsma—all musicians and DJs who made the trek from the Netherlands.

After the trip, Veneman gathered up all of the group's photos and posted them on a Web site served from his home computer. They shared them among the 313 list community, as well as "lowlands" (a Dutch techno culture list) and didn't think much more about the trip—that is, until they returned in 2000 after hearing "about Carl Craig doing a festival in May." Between these two trips, some friend or acquaintance in Detroit had dubbed the Dutch contingent "Techno Tourists," a name they embraced and reserved on the Web as "technotourist.org."

The Journey Home

What drew Veneman and crew back to Detroit in 2000 was, of course, a techno music event. But not some grassroots affair in tents pitched on rented farm property—this was the year of the very first Detroit Electronic Music Festival (DEMF). Established by Pop Culture Media and led by Carol Marvin (organizer for the Ford Detroit International Jazz Festival and Detroit-Montreux Jazz Festival before it), DEMF was planned to be the first major, mainstream showcase for electronic music in the city. Its impact was bigger and deeper than anyone could have imagined.

When the sun set on the first Saturday, enthusiasts, suburban visitors, city residents, and random passersby flocked to the free festival, converging on

Stacey Pullen's DJ set on the main stage. Hart Plaza was at or near capacity. The weather was perfect. Downtown Detroit came alive with strange, yet familiar sounds. What everyone slowly realized was that they were witnessing and participating in the reunion of the city with its long-lost, homegrown Wunderkind. Detroit finally "got" techno—it was emotional, magical, and as hyperbolic as you might imagine.

The reported numbers by city officials and the police department for that first weekend were a bit off the charts (as high as 1.5 million!), but it would take several years to come down from the high of such a successful launch to scrutinize attendance. It certainly *felt* like a million people had decided to soak up the music on the waterfront all at the same time. Emotion got the better of mathematics and logistics—quite the poetic *techno* ending to an improbable story.

The following year brought with it a new plot development. Though she had chosen Carl Craig to act as "artistic director" of the festival in 2000, Carol Marvin decided to fire him just before the opening day of the second DEMF. Marvin cited that Craig did not fulfill the terms of his contract, and Craig in turn sued (and lost) for defamation of character and breach of contract. But Craig seemed to have won "the popular vote," as banners and stickers bearing the slogans "I Support Carl Craig" and "DEMF = Carl Craig" were visible all weekend. And, to this day, the artistic direction and lineups of the first two festivals are regarded by many as the best.[7] "Even with all the politics and all the bullshit—the typical Detroit politics—I would never change it," said Craig. "It was great."[8]

Technotourist.org grew like a weed during the next festival, largely because it had decided to compile and host the dozens of after-parties that dotted the downtown map. Though the phrase "techno tourist" never caught on in a big way, it is a useful concept to replace that of the tribal or nomadic "raver." They created a blueprint for the next generation of techno fans, out to collect, overdocument, and share experiences. It might be reaching to say that they alone connected techno to the power of Web 2.0, but if nothing else, the techno tourists helped make it easier for more international visitors to descend on Detroit. Veneman remembers crossing into Canada and back during one of the festival weekends, and how literally *otherworldly* Detroit would become: "When I was the only Dutch guy and had to talk to customs—difficult, difficult. But we once went with two Dutch people, Ines from Germany and Jason from Australia. [Border security] asked if any of us were from outside the United States. We told him our nationalities and got a completely blank stare back. 'Drive on, please,' he said."

Incredibly, the music festival has lasted ten years, despite three changes in leadership and the woes of attracting and securing sponsors. In 2006 it might have fallen apart for good, if not for another entity born of Detroit's underground music scene. On the heels of the 2005 festival (then called F.U.S.E.:IN), producer Kevin Saunderson resigned with only a few months left before the next event. On March 23, the city gave the reins to Paxahau, who had produced the underground stage the prior year.

The official announcement of Paxahau as producer created almost as much excitement as when the official lineups are announced. The team was congratulated by many at that year's Winter Music Conference in Miami, and a few parties in Chicago that weekend stopped the music to announce Paxahau's involvement. Detroit's party scene had "arrived" in the same way techno artists did in 2000. Still, there was a lot of logic to the city's decision, given Paxahau's reputation and track record of handling increasingly larger events, such as the five parties they produced in and around the 2006 Super Bowl. Paxahau's Jason Huvaere was excited for sure, but also a textbook definition of "cautiously optimistic": "There were a lot of things that had to be calculated with great accuracy, or we were going to join the club [of short-lived festival producers]. We filed it down from the 1.5 million (of 2001). We just went to the venue and asked what the capacity was. To our surprise, we were the only ones who had asked that! [Hart Plaza is] rated for 45,000 people. It's always been in the book. The whole diagram needed to be adjusted."

In addition to simply "right-sizing" *Movement* (the festival's current name), Paxahau managed to do a lot of other things well, chief among them sound. Every year since 2006 has raised the bar in that regard, bringing top-notch sound to the Red Bull–sponsored stage hugging the waterfront, making the most of the Main stage's big expanse and finally figuring out the sonic puzzle that is the underground stage. They've leveraged their relationships with artists abroad and built on the stability of the festival's five years as a ticketed event. That may not stop some from complaining about ticket prices, especially 2008's single-day entrance fee of $25, but it's become hard to argue when Detroit can actually *count* on this festival happening. It's Paxahau's party now—a fact of which Huvaere is all too aware: "It takes about a month to come down from that event. Aside from the clean-up you have a lot of bills to pay, etcetera. By the time it hit us . . . the idea that this was not a temporary job, it was time to plan for the next one. It's non-stop. The communications have to be kept going year-round. [The year] 2005 was our last summer off."

For better or worse, techno has shed a lot of its mystique. There are no secret identities left to uncover, fewer hidden messages tucked in the run-out grooves. And now, party promoters who once searched for out-of-the-way venues and buildings are now out in the open. Moreover, techno has been documented and celebrated on many levels by this point. The result is that Detroit's street cred has become much larger than the boundaries of its streets.

Still Love in the Midwest

With a part of its "secret origin" set in a small town a half-hour's drive to the west, techno left an imprint just outside Detroit's borders that has continued to grow in parallel. Atkins, May, and Saunderson attending Belleville High School seemed like an anomaly ten years ago. Looking at the artists living and thriving in Washtenaw County today, it all seems like part of the plan.

From Belleville, Ypsilanti is much closer than Detroit—surely one of the reasons Juan Atkins attended Washtenaw Community College, where he would meet Rik Davis. Though their first Cybotron album, *Enter,* would be recorded in Ann Arbor (the original home of Pearl Sound), the concept for the band and much of its material was conceived in Ypsilanti, adjacent to the southeast. A few tracks were even recorded in the basement of TC's Speakeasy on Michigan Avenue—a bar and grill with a great reputation for live music.

The exchange of musicians, studios, and resources among Detroit, Ann Arbor, and Ypsilanti continued in the mid-1980s, as Kevin Saunderson attended Eastern Michigan University and used his fraternity as home base when Inner City was just getting off the ground. Still performing as "The Wizard," Jeff Mills also schooled legions of University of Michigan students when he was the resident DJ at the Nectarine Ballroom on Liberty Street.

College radio was no exception. Still wielding the kind of freeform power most radio dials will never encounter again, U of M's WCBN gave electronic dance music a comfortable place to rest in *Crush Collision,* a two-hour block of techno and its descendants. Currently hosted by Carlos Souffront and Todd Osborn, the show has aired every Thursday since 1990, quite a feat for an electronic music show on college radio. Brendan Gillen, a former host of the show and music director for WCBN, founded the Interdimensional Transmissions label in 1995 and performs with Erika Sherman (also a former director at the station) as Ectomorph, summoning their ominous brand of electro like a pair of Lovecraftian protagonists.

One avid *Crush* listener was Sam Valenti IV, an art history student from 1998 to 2002. Valenti founded the Ghostly International label, signed its first artists, and watched it thrive all before he graduated. It would be easy to forgive someone raised on techno music and access to area record shops for being a copycat or for licensing as many Detroit artists as possible. Valenti has built a successful and highly respected label without falling into either trap. Ghostly has roots in Detroit and techno to be sure, but their roster is a paragon of eclecticism, something Valenti isn't sure is readily available the way it was for him: "The genre-bending aspects of Detroit musicians and DJs were really the inspiration—[telling us] that it was okay to play different kinds of stuff. The radio DJs . . . the peak of the mixes where they'd play drum & bass, ghetto-tech and hip-hop. I really liked that. People who really gave a shit about music were all around."

Matthew Dear was Ghostly's first artist, a transplanted Texan Valenti met at a house party Dear was DJing at. Nearly every other artist was living in Ann Arbor or Ypsilanti at the label's onset. Strangely enough, outside of Dear, few were fellow University of Michigan students. It was as if Ghostly's namesake icon was a signal that awakened all the talent in a fifteen-mile radius. One such talent was Todd Osborn, who was already making music on his own and connecting dots in the scene as the proprietor of the Dubplate Pressure record store. His first release didn't come until a split twelve-inch with the DMX Crew in 2002, but he has been a consistent player throughout the label's development.

Osborn also introduced Sam Valenti to Tadd Mullinix, aka Dabrye. When Mullinix came onboard, Ghostly needed a sister label in Spectral Sound to help give some distance between the more dance floor–targeted material Matthew Dear was working on. Still, all of these decisions were being made among a network of acquaintances all based some distance *away* from Detroit—and from a dorm room.

[Being in Ann Arbor] was kind of a statement that "you could be anywhere."
Ann Arbor is a college town, very liberal and special. But it's a Midwestern town,
and doesn't have anything that much more impressive than other college towns
in America, so to speak. I thought [Ghostly's stance] was a metaphor for you
can do it too . . . you don't have to be on the coasts or have a "big" artist. You
don't have to be "connected."

In fact, Ghostly leaned on one local artist quite heavily at the start. Four
of its first five releases all featured Mullinix under different aliases, including the "Charles Manier" name used on 2002's *Disco Nouveau* compilation. This was a curatorial exercise of sorts, a juxtaposition of old disco

and electro styles that gained the label a lot of media attention. Though most dance-centric labels stick to twelve-inch single releases, Matthew Dear hit it big on Spectral with his 2003 album on Spectral, *Leave Luck to Heaven*. After a critically acclaimed compilation and a successful album debut from its first artist, one might say the label had momentum by this point.

Ghostly also signed what fans of electronic music might remember as "bands," a concept that was once foreign outside the force-fit of electronica's stadium-rock approach. Kill Memory Crash and Midwest Product (which begat Post Prior, which begat Ben Benjamin) were early signs that Ghostly International was not going to do things like any label before them, except perhaps some of the highly curated British labels like Manchester's Factory Records. Basically, Ghostly and Spectral never milked any one formula, going against the conventional wisdom in the music industry. Valenti is visibly proud of this fact—that the crazy jumble of influences that fed into techno and Ghostly's beginnings have produced equally unpredictable outcomes.

> Ghostly is modeled as a label for fans of good music. We don't have a genre fan base the way that even a Stones Throw show will have a hip-hop base; we have a real amalgam of people that like us. From techno people to art school people to hip-hop people—and I like it that way. It makes it difficult, because you don't have a guaranteed five thousand kids that are going to buy something, but at least you can ebb and flow with the time. You're not going to dead-end, you're not going to *trip-hop*.

By the turn of the twenty-first century, two things were certain: the legacy of Detroit was living on and thriving at home and abroad, and the confusion surrounding what exactly "techno" was hadn't subsided. But there were the inklings of change in the over-segmented music industry dynamic. Attitudes were changing—and forces like Delsin and Ghostly proved that you could follow Detroit techno's lead without having to invoke its entire history or copy it outright. Unlike the indignities the city of Detroit continues to suffer, it was clear that techno's history would not be humiliated.

7

Beyond the Dance

The Future Sound
of Techno, 1999–?

WHAT BECOMES PAINFULLY OBVIOUS IS THE NARROW PERCEPTION
OF THOSE IN POWER TO SEE THAT CHANGE IS A GOOD THING. IF
ANYTHING, WHAT THIS MUSIC REPRESENTS IS A CHANGE, A RAPID
DEVELOPMENT TOWARDS SOMETHING ELSE. ADMITTEDLY MORE ALIEN,
MORE FACELESS, ELECTRONIC MUSIC REPRESENTS THE EVOLUTION
OF MUSIC. THIS IS PERHAPS NOT THE DEATH OF ROCK 'N' ROLL
BUT ITS RECONSTRUCTION.
TODD ROBERTS AND TAMARA PALMER, "THE NEXT BIG THING,"
URB, NO. 53, P. 67

So what now? Techno has made the journey from Detroit neighborhoods to all seven continents, from the underground to the mainstream, and from high school party politics to the "peace, love, unity, respect" mottoes of rave culture. Will it continue fighting its way through the mass media and the lowest common denominator? And how does techno measure its progress in the twenty-first century, now that it has saturated nearly every corner of the globe?

Even as 1997's electronica craze fades into history, it's clear that the United States is still techno's toughest, harshest obstacle. In attempting to reach wider audiences here, the music has lost too much through too many compromises. And after several attempts to include techno in its plans, the U.S. music industry hasn't really conceded much in the process. In other words, techno has to face the reality that in the United States, it's not destined to run in the same circles as "rock" or "jazz."

Techno represents a radical departure from traditional marketing techniques and the promotion of personalities—one that may or may not add to the total experience. The only way techno can work with or inside larger entities is if it is allowed room to grow and if there is a concerted effort to educate audiences and industry alike. Giving techno the autonomy it already takes for granted is a strange proposition, but sooner or later some label will figure out a way to make it work. One short-lived example came from a seemingly unlikely source: the Sony Corporation. Sony has a wide and worldly view and, at least in Japan, it recognized techno as a powerful movement with an agenda and impetus all its own.

In January 1994, a small part of the foreign music department at Sony Entertainment Japan (where big names like Mariah Carey are handled) began releasing catalog material from R&S, Warp, and Rising High. This led to the establishment of Sony Techno later that year, a department that today licenses material from Transmat, Warp, and Rephlex, as well as Japanese labels like Denku and newer Japanese artists. According to Sony A&R man Masakazu Hiroishi, it wasn't an easy five years.

> At the beginning, the [Japanese] market for techno was still very immature and small. It was like trying to make a road in a jungle. It was more about educating the whole music industry of this new genre before we could even start promoting individual artists. It was essential to work closely with press, promoters, and retail to plan detailed articles on techno, organizing parties at clubs and arranging retail campaigns to create the basis for this music genre.

It is debatable whether this type of major label techno department is a realistic possibility in the United States, even with Americans slowly inching toward acceptance of the genre. As Hiroishi explained:

> Personally, I would very much like to see such an entity happen in Sony USA or in any of the major U.S. record companies, but I am not very optimistic about it. The techno acts who are successful in the United States now are not pure techno but are more of crossovers between rock or hip-hop. It would be possi-

ble for an indie label to team up with a major record company to enforce the distributions, as it is often seen in the hip-hop industry. However, techno requires special care and handling. Some of the attractions of this music can be weakened along the way when it is handled by too many people.

Since major labels never fully stepped up with practical approaches, the responsibility for techno's future success shifted back to the underground and smaller labels. As shown by entities like Submerge, the underground has come to understand its business and niche market existence. But even with digital tools available to speed up and narrow the focus of distribution, the only mechanism small labels have for cultivating a techno audience is word of mouth. Even in the era of large-scale social networks such as Facebook and a plethora of digital record stores, there's nothing that can replace the major label marketing push of old. Ironically, this may be just fine with techno's producers, many of whom aren't expecting their records to have an impact in every country—especially the United States. One such artist is Alan Oldham, who shut down his first globally oriented label, Generator, in 1996. For his newer Pure Sonik label, Oldham opted for a more practical approach.

> I don't care if America's not into my music, because America wasn't into Trane [John Coltrane] or Miles [Miles Davis] either. I think [it will have] a subtle growth—it's going to be one of those things where you wake up one day and you're going to find it will have cracked in some way. I'm not going to sell 500,000 units any time soon, I can tell you that. [But] if I can get a solid 5,000 people to buy my record, I'll be all right forever. Remember, [it was] back around 1988 that [the] Windham Hill shit and the whole New Age movement was at the apex of its popularity, and now it's kind of settled into the people who like it. [Artists like] John Tesh, Mark Isham, [and] Tuck and Patti live off that cult, and that's where you want to be. To me, techno is only going to be that big.

There's no complete explanation for the stacked decks and uphill battles techno artists have faced in the United States. But there is one way to look at how the United States became "Island America," or how we can often be reluctant or downright loath to accept foreign ideas or attitudes—a comparison with soccer interest from the 1970s on. There's a parallel to the acceptance of techno at every step: disco fever coinciding with the heyday of the National American Soccer League and Brazilian soccer star Pelé in the 1970s, burgeoning professional soccer leagues and young techno scenes everywhere *except* the United States in the 1980s and 1990s—all the way up to Americans' newfound interest in "electronica" and Major League Soccer in the late 1990s. It's as if the ball has finally been passed back stateside, and we're still fighting the temptation to use our hands.

Dear Genre

It takes great patience to understand the fragmented landscape of today's electronic music—especially if one plans to purchase music products, rather than experience it in the context of a club or party. As much as techno is a sum of musical influences, it has also divided into an infinite number of substrata, which are nearly impossible to trace. The easiest way to start is by looking at the "stronger" genres that have emerged—those that have developed into full-fledged musical movements of their own and are not only distinct but have proven out over time.

One of the most futuristic-sounding styles is that of "drum & bass."[1] One explanation of drum & bass is that it is an accelerated evolution of hip-hop, brought on by the advancements and prevalence of digital sampling technology. But this description obscures a complicated evolution similar to that of techno. Part Jamaican "dub," part hip-hop, part techno, and all British, drum & bass reflects both the cumulative history of electronic dance music and its unexplored possibilities.

It's no accident that drum & bass has captured so much attention and analysis. Its absorption of and residual effects on any form of music it touches is a fascinating process. With a signature sound resonating just inside our comprehension, drum & bass is centered on disjointed, fibrillating drum patterns and subsonic, rumbling basslines. This "basic" rhythmic framework has given an array of other genres and artists a new context in which to be heard. Drum & bass has worked its way into Soul Coughing's brutal beat poetry, the R&B productions of Timbaland and Missy Elliot, and even the melodies of Brazilian composer Antonio Carlos Jobim. In recent years, it has also become a preset, generic "music bed" for sports highlight reels and television commercials. Like the Detroit techno scene in the mid-1990s, it also went back underground.

Drum & bass has also attracted attention with its surreal division and coexistence of different tempos: basslines generally clock in at half the

beats-per-minute ratio of the reconstituted breakbeats (80 to 160 bpm, for example). "You had hard-core/breakbeat circa 1991," says Dego McFarlane of 4Hero and London's Reinforced Records. "Prodigy [along with N-joi and Altern 8, among the more visible] was a part of the scene, though back then it was around 125–130 bpm—now it's at 160 and up."

There are almost as many drum & bass subcategories as there are drum & bass records, as even the slightest new musical direction seems to generate a new, artificially created subgenre, raising ire among many of its original producers. A superfluous lexicon nearly choked the life out of Britain's most interesting musical export. As McFarlane exclaims, "As far as terms go, I couldn't give a toss about any of them. [Proceeds to ramble off a dozen or so combinations, including jungle, hard core, step, breakbeat, ambient, and dark. . . . They're all a load of crap."

McFarlane's viewpoint comes from having witnessed the rapid evolution of dance music and from helping several of today's drum & bass artists start their careers. Many innovators have passed through Reinforced Records, including Ray Keith & Doc Scott, Younghead, L Double, DJ Peshay, Nookie, and Leon Mar (aka Arcon 2). The label's best-known drum & bass progeny is Goldie, a former graffiti artist and break-dancer from Walsall, England. Born in 1966 to a Scottish mother and Jamaican father, Goldie was put up for adoption and has never revealed his true identity to the press. By 1991, he had migrated from the hip-hop culture of his youth to that of the emerging breakbeat scene. His debut singles on Reinforced —"Killa Muffin" and "Darkrider"—came in 1992, under the "Rufige Kru" pseudonym. Eventually, Goldie's own imprint, Metalheadz, began occupying more and more of his time, though he still managed to collaborate on several Reinforced projects simultaneously, including a 1995 collaboration with A Guy Called Gerald titled "The Two G's." Metalheadz eventually became a launching pad for yet another wave of drum & bass artists, including Source Direct, Optical, Peshay, and Photek.

Working with producers McFarlane, Rob Playford, Dillinja, and Mark Mac, Goldie's recordings (such as 1995's "Timeless") were elevated into the U.K. spotlight. The combination of these choice musical associations and his persona as a "21st Century B-Boy" made a major label deal inevitable.[2] In 1995, Goldie signed a contract with London Records and an album soon followed. *Timeless* was drum & bass's watershed moment, galvanizing interest in its underground movement and exposing the mainstream to the possibilities of pop-music crossovers. Carved out of the twenty-one-minute title song "Timeless,"[3] the single "Inner City Life" featured vocals by Diane Charlemagne and led the way for dozens of drum & bass/vocalist experiments. It was the cornerstone of the alt-pop group Everything But the Girl's evolution on their album *Walking Wounded* and lives on today in tracks like those from the collaborations of Nu:Tone and Natalie Williams on Hospital Records.

Like techno, drum & bass carries with it a long history at this point. It also follows suit in that a lot of original producers are still actively producing music, if not just on the DJ circuit. This can tend to mask the contributions of new artists on the scene. "[In] dubplate culture (where the freshness of your selection is critical), it's inevitable that those with the highest profiles and longest histories are going to be top of the game," says Nu:Tone's Dan Gresham. "It's spectacularly hard for people to reach a similar level of notoriety."

Drum & bass also seems to have reached the same level of maturity and resilience to conquer the plagues of assigning genres to its every move. There is something more satisfying about music when it does not have a name, or knowing that a specific designation has stood the test of time. Ghostly's Sam Valenti had his specter (no pun intended) in avoiding the dead end of trip-hop. Dance music defined by its ever-increasing speed inevitably runs out of gas or hits the wall. There is a lesson for listeners and club-goers in leaving the dividing of records to the DJs who have to lug them around. Gresham:

> D&B [drum & bass] has gone through a few periods where it's looked like it will truly fragment (à la House), but each time it's pulled itself back together again. One of the great strengths of the scene is its ability to incorporate so many different styles and flavors under the same umbrella. The pigeon-holing obsession primarily comes from journalists and forum-heroes, and generally only serves a negative purpose ("I can't stand *neuro-liquid*—I'm only into *darkside-wobble*").

While techno, house, and drum & bass were often in danger of becoming a federation of balkanized genres, artists and DJs also took a turn to the basics, mining classic disco and other inspirations. The same crowd ready with a new genre name for each successive move are the same critics, fans, and promoters that would label such a move "retro." Consider the persistent electro movement or even the turntablists breaking off from "mainstream" hip-hop. Time is no more useful in defining these concepts than the genre names themselves. Consider author Jon Savage's assessment of the styles that were literally stitched together to form the fabric of punk: "As these styles began to unravel within popular culture, pop's linear time was shattered forever: there would be no more unified 'movements,' but tribes, as pop time became forever multiple. Postmodern."[4]

One of the more poorly named genres is yet another outlet for the evolution of techno. Post-rock, as self-described, is an extension of and departure from traditional rock structures—usually with the same outward veneer of a band. Strangely (or perhaps fittingly), one of the hubs of post-rock activity is Michigan, home of bands such as Livonia's His Name Is Alive (signed to the legendary English indie label 4AD) and Windy & Carl. Unfortunately, aside from a handful of remixes, post-rock has not yet connected with any of Detroit's techno producers.

Post-rock seems to be in a unique position, poised at a nexus of creative possibilities and an understanding of the industry's ups and downs. Many post-rock bands are more like collectives of adventurous musicians who settle into a groove after a bedouin-like existence of moving from one group to the next. Making the most of this position is Chicago's Tortoise, formed in 1990 by members of Eleventh Dream Day, Chicago Underground Orchestra, the Poster Children, Bastro, the Tar Babies, and about a dozen others. John McEntire, who seems to anchor the group, also serves as its main drummer/percussionist, though being a "band" is about the last thing on Tortoise's agenda. "It was just this collection of people," he told *The Wire* in 1996. "Along with that, the instruments that most of us were proficient with didn't necessarily include playing the guitar or singing. So we decided: why bother with that?"[5]

As in techno, musical gear plays a central role in Tortoise's post-rock: the group's live shows look more like reconstructions of studio sessions, with every last nook and cranny occupied by a different unconventional instrument (it's not uncommon for two members to be playing vibraphone simultaneously). Steel guitars and marimbas share space with synths and drum machines, and are used to create a mixture of unwound dance music, dub, and film scores.[6] At best, Tortoise is a snapshot of a moving target. The group's side projects, almost as numerous as its former bands, coexist peacefully and even progressively; individual compositions migrate from one group to the next, picking up and discarding components along the way. Tortoise's 1998 single "Jetty," for example, is essentially a reworked narrative from Isotope 217's "La Jetee."

In almost every aspect, the bands like Tortoise deconstructed rock and made electronic music acceptable, if not integral, to their sound. The independent ("indie") rock community seems to have noticed in the years since "post-rock" and has embraced electronics more readily and completely. In some ways it's the fusion of the independent streaks in both rock and techno. The evolved approaches of artists such as Postal Service, Four Tet, Caribou, and Broadcast defy genre definitions with a new rigor.

Jazz Is the Teacher

An evolution in the structure of classic techno itself has been spearheaded by jazz fusions and infusions, by groups with their roots in electro (the Black Dog, Plaid, and 808 State), and by younger American artists weaned on the complexities of Atkins, May, and Craig. Artists such as Dan Curtin, Morgan Geist, and Titonton Duvante read into the complicated patterns and feelings of Detroit's music and matched them with changes in tempo, instrumentation, and texture. In doing so, they found ways to be funky, forceful, and quirky (almost to a fault), and yet still make their records workable for DJs—at least those talented enough to work with smaller sections of grooves rather than the typical extended mixes of dance music.

Efforts to expand the structure of techno are also producing myriad combinations with jazz music. Jazz is one music genre from which techno seems to take all kinds of cues,[7] and in fact the cultural parallels between techno and bebop in particular are striking: both originated with African American artists, both faced early resistance from U.S. audiences and traveled to Europe for greater acceptance, and both became popularized (some might say watered down) by white artists.

Given the improvisational character of jazz, combinations with techno seem nearly impossible. But through the work of various producers, ranging from powerhouses like Underground Resistance to more obscure acts like Gregory Watts's GFQ, a lot of progress has been made in finding common elements between the two. Musicians like Carl Craig and Kirk DeGiorgio have even taken a literal approach, incorporating session players into their recordings and live performances. Craig, for example, enlisted jazz bassist Rodney Whitaker and percussionist Francisco Mora for his groundbreaking Inner-zone Orchestra.

While all of these jazz-related projects are ambitious, the most impressive still seem to be coming from studio-born projects, such as David Moufang's loose collaboration Conjoint, all of Jonah Sharp's work with Spacetime Continuum, and experiments with 3/4 time signatures in the work of Jason (Velocette) Williams and on Ian O'Brien's *Desert Scores*. These artists seem to sense that technology gives techno the same kind of freedom that bebop brought to jazz in the 1950s.

Radical experimentation has also come to infect techno's structures of beat, melody, and rhythm. Techno's traditional 4/4 time signature, while easiest for nightclubbers (not to mention most of the Western Hemisphere) to understand, often requires the function of melody to become subservient to that of rhythm. Though experiments in separating the two have made for some great music (such as Plastikman's more chitinous beats and select ambient records), they've also shown that techno loses its definition without a balance between the two. A release called *Acid Brass*, for example, which includes techno and acid house hits from the late 1980s played by a traditional brass band, showed that that Derrick May's classic "Strings of Life" doesn't sound nearly as impressive on brass band instruments; its house-style piano melody and sampled strings sound painfully repetitive without May's 909 programming.

Perhaps as a direct response to the subdivision of dance music, but more likely a semiconscious shift in artistic style, there is also a strain of techno that has survived by shedding characteristics rather than collecting them. Detroit began breaking its music down and building it back up about five years ago, a process that became known as "minimal" techno. At the forefront and producing some of the most interesting recombinant forms are Daniel Bell and Robert Hood.

Bell started his Accelerate label in November 1992, a few months before the end of Cybersonik's project with Plus 8. Creating a distinct sound that reflected his interests was difficult, especially with only four pieces of equipment, but he eventually settled into an approach that worked. "Even when I was doing hip-hop I was known for having a sparse style," he says. "It took me a while to develop that with techno." Bell is a bit critical of the term with which his work has been branded. "I never liked minimalism as an art movement—at all," he says. "There was nothing interesting in it, it was just an 'arty' thing to do—a superficial way of trying to get someone's attention."

And indeed, this is where the comparison between Detroit's music and other forms of minimalism falls flat: Detroit's variety was more an exercise in reverse engineering, a quest to find the lost funk in techno music. As Robert Hood explains:

> I think Dan and I both realized that something was missing—an element . . . in what we both know as techno. It sounded great from a production standpoint, but there was a "jack" element in the [old] structure. People would complain that there's no funk, no feeling in techno anymore, and the easy escape is to put a vocalist and some piano on top to fill that emotional gap. I thought it was time for a return to the original underground.

At the same time Bell was finessing his new approach, Hood was slowly shifting out of his role in Underground Resistance. Working independently of one another, Bell and Hood created milestones in the so-called minimalist movement: Bell with "Losing Control" (Peacefrog)[8] and Hood with his *Internal Empire* album (Tresor/BMG) and *Minimal Nation* EP (Axis) (all released in 1994).[9]

Hood's and Bell's sparse production styles have helped create one definition of "minimalist" techno—the other coming from a style based on a reduction of the "song" component to mere fractions of one bar. By cramming notes into smaller spaces, techno seems to become synonymous with repetition—one of the characteristics that generally turns people off from listening to dance music. One of the artists who has taken this style past listeners' reservations and to new levels is Jeff Mills. Mills creates deceptively dense, almost baroque orchestrations on his Axis and Purpose Maker labels, including the 1991 EP *Tranquilizer,* which he recorded with Hood as the group H&M (short for "Hood and Mills").

Mills is a consummate techno artist, to the point where his Detroit background is almost irrelevant. His work as a DJ has made him a "citizen of the world" in a record-toting, frequent flyer sort of way. Not that he hasn't earned it. By staying involved with every last detail of the recording, mastering, packaging, and design of his records and CDs, Mills saturates each release with imagery (Man Ray–style photography set against elegant black, gray, and gold designs) and elliptical sentences constructed in the same ultra-compressed mode as his music: "As barriers fall around the world the need to understand others and the way they live, think, and dream is a task that is nearly impossible to imagine without theory and explanation. and as we approach the next century with hope and prosperity, this need soon becomes a necessity rather than a recreational urge. theories and subjects of substance is the elementary element that fuels the minds within our axis."[10]

But Mills tends to downplay all of the attention he has received from fans and the press for his experimentation with techno. As he told the English magazine *Magic Feet* in 1998, "We're still too far, way too far from understanding all the things that could be done with this music."[11]

Desktop Robotics

One of the best things to happen to techno in the latter half of the 1990s was that it began to catch up to the future it had been serenading for years. The techno rebels embraced technologies beyond synthesizers and sequencers and, in the process, finally shed the ironically limiting term "postmodern" to become right at home in the present—which, in the information age, is way more than most of us can handle.

Unlike punk, which had fanzines to support its existence outside the mainstream, the wealth of information available about techno music—its artists, labels, and lifestyle—is too much to transmit via Xerox. Instead, techno artists have turned to the Internet as a tool for spreading event-based information. As the only place where techno's urgency can be emulated in real time and cataloged for future enthusiasts, the Net has become critical to techno's development. And as journalist Hari Kunzru points out, the Internet will only continue to disseminate techno and its progeny: "The number of musical styles seems to be doubling faster than computer processor speeds, governed by some as-yet-unknown dance-floor version of Moore's Law. The Net will speed up this research work even further. When musicians in Japan have instant access to the ebbs and flows of the U.K. underground (and vice versa), the rate of innovation will increase exponentially."[12]

The easiest place to trace the parallel growth of both techno and the Internet is Hyperreal,[13] a Web-based compendium and resource for electronic dance music and its various cultures. Hyperreal started as a simple node, created by Brian Behlendorf at Stanford University in 1992. This was well before the explosion of Internet usage ushered in by the Web, and the server was limited to text interfaces used by early adopters and those lucky enough to work or study at a networked institution.

A Google search for "techno culture" today will offer up hundreds of thousands of hits, but for many years, Hyperreal brought together many disparate rave movements, music-making resources, and some of the earliest streaming audio sites. Techno was one of the first genres to embrace the many digital alternatives to the FM band, and English techno group the Future Sound of London (FSOL) was one of the first to recognize the power of real Web "presence." In the mid-1990s they streamed live concerts from their studio to radio stations via high-speed ISDN lines and redefined the "performance" angle in the process.[14]

Get the Balance Right

Techno has grown up with a sense of optimism and future possibilities, and its practitioners seem to be far less hesitant than Toffler's techno rebels.

Still, at techno's core lies the struggle to retain the human element in its music. Whether this comes through unlocking the "warmth" of old analog gear, chord progressions, or the tactile connection to vinyl, techno has always struck the best and most interesting balance. The real danger seems to lie with fetishism—when techno's nostalgia and romanticism cross the line and inhibit its growth. Finding equilibrium may sound like a boring pursuit, but for techno it means existing at the center of a number of worlds, extremes, and paradoxes. Rather than any one particular sound, techno is more of a mind-set, having to do with the fantasizing and philosophizing of Derrick May and Juan Atkins as kids. This is where techno will always find its strength.

If techno is to succeed in the next decade, it must find a similar equilibrium when it comes to building a real audience in its home country. In addition to staying in the middle of both technological and musical convergence, techno labels (both large and small) need to remain nimble and to consider the possibilities of an eclectic artist roster, like Craig's Planet E. It's no accident that Planet E at one time was the Detroit label "properly" integrated into the American market, thanks in part to a distribution deal with Caroline Records.

Artist development, sorely lacking in dance music for the last twenty years, also needs to take root in all countries, not just the United States. Hundreds of artists have haphazardly taken that responsibility upon themselves, with mixed results. Without creating an environment of long-term growth, few of techno's pioneers are likely to receive the recognition they deserve. More than a decade ago, some labels were seeing definite possibilities for techno to be given the proper "room" to develop. Said Astralwerks's Wohelski at the time:

> I would only be able to pay an artist x amount of dollars as an advance on a project, but they would probably make more money on the back end from their royalties. I'd be interested in a multiple album deal or an album deal with options —[a deal that] shows some commitment to the artist. Hopping from European label x to y to z—just to get paid—isn't going to do anything for you as a career artist. If you are serious about breaking into the U.S. market, you have to put in the time and the effort. Although you may deserve their respect, you need to tell them why they need to respect you. I personally am not interested in ownership; I'm interested in artist development, because that's what this country needs

right now. This music comes from America and there's a wealth of talent in their own backyard that's not being exposed.

As for the running of large independent labels, there are few success stories like that of Submerge. And in fact, a scaling down to new, smaller labels has definitely been the trend—Richie Hawtin, for example, shifted his focus to his Minus label in 1998. As Hawtin explained:

> You learn better who you are, what you are, and how to better present that and present it creatively. [With Minus], we wanted to slow it [the pace] down and try new things. Just like Jeff [Mills] does [with] his Purpose Maker and Axis things—he is Axis and Axis is Jeff Mills. Whether it's a record release or an art exhibit or whatever, it's Jeff. That's where the people who see the bigger picture now are positioning themselves.

Techno is about the individual—the individual and his or her entanglements with technology. And at the rate technology is moving and changing, there are so many different ways that you can express yourself creatively. It's a full-time job just doing that. Maybe we can prove that this music can live in an independent mode and stand for itself . . . show the majors how it can be put out to society. Because in the last ten years, even though it's an independent thing, for the most part it's been run with smaller versions of big record companies.

To watch techno progress, one needs to keep an eye on the smallest of details rather than the big picture. No one could have predicted the eruption of drum & bass out of clever sequencing and sampling, nor did synth manufacturer Roland ever dream of the sounds techno would summon from the machines it created to emulate real drums and bass guitars. And Detroit's role as a cultural mecca caught everyone by surprise—even most of its producers. One needs to follow the optimists: artists, DJs, producers and promoters who transcend the politics and stifling framework of the record business, and who are still seeking new ways to connect to other human beings. And Jeff Mills thinks we've only heard a small fraction of what's possible: "I think there isn't enough experimentation in music as a whole. Considering all the things that can be explored with computers and programming software, what we're hearing from the music industry is quite disappointing. And the idea that people can only accept simple things is a insult. I believe techno music should endorse new thinking and new approaches to what can be done with sound and rhythm." Though they haven't recorded an Underground Resistance record together in years, Mike Banks echoes Mills's statements. "The age of people being open-minded never went away," he says. "The ears are still there."

Notes

Chapter 1

1. Organic was held in California's San Bernardino National Forest on June 22, 1996, and featured live performances by the Orb, the Chemical Brothers, Orbital, Underworld, Meat Beat Manifesto, and Loop Guru.
2. Interstitials are program or station identification segments that are used as buffers between the program and commercials.
3. Throughout the book, quotes from informal interviews I conducted and from conversations with various people in the music industry will be uncited.
4. Patrick Reilly, "Will Pulsing 'Techno' Sound Rev Up Music Business?" *Wall Street Journal*, January 27, 1997.
5. This hybrid would later be refined and renamed "big beat."
6. Andrew Parks, "Entertain Us: The State of Electronica," *XLR8R.com*, April 30, 2008.
7. Mark Sinker and Tim Barr, *The History of House*, ed. Chris Kempster (London: Sanctuary Publishing, 1996), 95.
8. Pascal Bussy, *Kraftwerk: Man, Machine and Music* (Wembley: SAF Publishing, 1993), 54.
9. Baker was also notable for introducing the English group New Order to the "Funhouse" sound heard in its 1983 club classic "Confusion."
10. The two are often simply referred to as "Ralf & Florian," probably because they released an album of the same name in 1973.
11. Stuart Cosgrove, "Seventh City Techno," *The Face*, no. 97 (May 1988): 86.
12. Alvin Toffler, *The Third Wave* (New York: Bantam, 1980), 15.

Chapter 2

1. Detroit's "Seventh City" alias comes from the fact that it boasted the nation's seventh-largest population through 1990.
2. Bounded roughly by Eight Mile Road to the north, Fenkell Avenue (Five Mile Road) to the south, Woodward Avenue to the east, and Telegraph Road to the west, northwest Detroit is a residential area that has historically been one of the city's most affluent. In 1979, this area's average median family income was 34 percent higher than that of the rest of the city.
3. Ciabittino was named after a shoe store in the upscale suburb of Birmingham, Michigan.
4. Direct Drive was named for the type of turntable that spins via a series of gears, uninhibited by belts or events triggered by the tonearm.
5. This party would also inspire the first "techno" record of sorts, as we'll learn later (see page 28).
6. In the 1980s, Cass Tech and Henry Ford (two Detroit high schools) were attended mainly by youth from northwest Detroit.
7. Electro now threatens to eclipse techno as the chief dance music export of Detroit.
8. DREAD stands for Detroit Rockers Engaged in the Abolition of Disco.
9. Yet another disco variant, hi-NRG was characterized by faster tempos and vocals that often didn't match the beat structure.
10. *Suspiria* in turn inspired Detroit artist Carl Craig to record a dance track of the same name years later in 1991.
11. "Problèmes D'Amour" was so popular on Detroit's urban contemporary stations that it was not uncommon to hear it played in the *daytime.*
12. Jon Savage, *England's Dreaming: Anarchy, Sex Pistols, Punk Rock and Beyond* (New York: St. Martin's Press, 1992), 81.
13. The catalog number for the Capriccio pressing of "Sharevari," P-928, was even chosen to pay homage to the ultimate preppy/yuppie vehicle, the Porsche 928.
14. The confusion probably started with the image of this white "rock" band fronted by two African American singers (Sweet Pea Atkinson and [Sir] Harry Bowens).
15. Believe it or not, "Flamethrower Rap" was a rap version of the J. Geils Band's disco tour de force "Flamethrower."
16. Collier was often behind the mixing desk with Don Fagenson of the group Was (Not Was). The two were often credited as the "Wasmopolitan Mixing Squad."
17. Alan Oldham, also known as DJ-T1000, was a champion of techno on Detroit public radio in the late 1980s and early 1990s.
18. "Kaos" was also the name of one of May's first recordings as Rhythim Is Rhythm, a name he recorded under in the late 1980s.
19. Neil Ollivierra, "Reality Slap" (Detroit, 1992), 13.
20. The 1960 U.S. Census listed Detroit's population as 1,670,144.
21. Jerry Herron, *AfterCulture: Detroit and the Humiliation of History* (Detroit: Wayne State University Press, 1993), 88.

22. This site can be found at http://bhere.com/ruins/.

23. *Robocop* was one of many 1980s films set in Detroit but *not* shot in the city.

24. Two of Detroit's largest television stations are headquartered in the suburbs.

25. Devil's Night is the traditionally mischievous night before Halloween. In Detroit, Devil's Night has often been an excuse for widespread arson.

26. This segment did not go unnoticed by Detroit's techno community. One of Alan Oldham's first recordings shared the show's title and actually sampled its dialogue.

27. Herron, *AfterCulture,* 27.

Chapter 3

1. The liner notes for *Enter* list the record as "Recorded at Randy Howe's parents' house while they were elsewhere."

2. Bill Brown, "Cybotron's Politically Explicit, Do-It-Yourself Approach Leads to Success," *Ann Arbor News,* October 15, 1983, B3.

3. Actually recorded under the "Channel One" pseudonym, "Technicolor" wound up being a DJ favorite and was even sampled by Seattle rapper/producer Sir Mix-A-Lot for "Baby Got Back."

4. The a cappella version of this song, "Time, Space, Transmat," extended the transportation metaphor beyond modern physics, hinting at a way to literally move freely in time and space. Detroit techno artist Derrick May would later take the word "transmat" to name his own record label.

5. Additionally, a "transmat" was a teleportation device on the sci-fi television show *Dr. Who.*

6. The lyrics were undoubtedly ad-libbed, as May has always held that everyone in the studio was drunk except for him.

7. A flange is a specific time-based effect used in recording that stimulates multiple instruments (or audio signals) played simultaneously. Delay and phase changes are used to cancel out certain frequencies, producing a characteristic "whoosh" sound.

8. The full Deep Space lineup included "Magic" Juan Atkins, Derrick "Mayday" May, Eddie "Flashin'" Fowlkes, Kevin "Master Reese" Saunderson, Art "Pumpin'" Payne, and Keith "Mixin'" Martin.

9. As a play on "Maurice," Saunderson often used "Reese" or "Master Reese" as stage names.

10. The two were known simply as "Reese and Santonio."

11. The Electrifying Mojo's radio show (sometimes called "The Midnight Funk Association," depending on which station was airing the show) has been on no fewer than six Detroit-area stations since the mid-1970s: WGPR, WJLB, WHYT, WTWR (Monroe), WMXD, and WCHB. During one dry spell Johnson even offered content over the phone at 976-MOJO.

12. At the height of both Johnson's and Prince's popularity, from 1983 to 1985, the Purple Rain Tour stayed in Detroit for seven shows. Prince also performed a special concert at Cobo Hall to celebrate his birthday in 1986.

13. Electrifying Mojo, *The Mental Machine* (Detroit: Charles Johnson, 1993).

14. The only time Mills got a memo from programming was when he started playing Public Enemy, which was deemed too controversial at the time. Eventually, Mills found a way to mix it back in.
15. Jeff Mills was also a founding member of the "industrial" music group Final Cut.

Chapter 4

1. Speak & Spell was an educational toy manufactured by Mattel that produced synthesized speech. The toy's speech was incorporated into both "Techno Music" and *Computer World.*
2. Virgin's kickoff party for the compilation featured Boy George and Jazzie (Soul II Soul) B, among others.
3. Adrenalin MOD, aka Darren Mohammed, Richie Fermie, and Darren Bird, is one of acid house's forgotten talents.
4. Louise Gray, "Paradise Revisited," *City Limits* (June 30 – July 7, 1988): 21.
5. Stuart Cosgrove, "Seventh City Techno," *The Face,* no. 97 (May 1988): 88.
6. ZTT is Zang Tuum Tumb, the same label that housed Frankie Goes to Hollywood and the Art of Noise, among others.
7. Luckily, Craig did rescue some of these sessions, repurposing them later on his Retroactive and Planet E labels.
8. Before all was said and done, May and Craig would get to work on the last S'Express album, *Intercourse,* in 1990.
9. DMC stands for Disco Mix Club, a DJ organization that is now international.
10. Sweet Exorcist was a pseudonym for Cabaret Voltaire's Richard H. Kirk, an artist who had seen new potential in a sound that he had helped develop.
11. FFRR stands for Full Frequency Range Recordings.
12. Derrick May, interview by Brent Bambry, *Brave New Waves,* CBC radio, Montreal, 1990.
13. In fact, Detroit was relatively late in forming its own rave scene, with the first signs appearing in 1992.

Chapter 5

1. "White labels," or early releases of records, were popular in the underground dance community of the 1990s. White labels were so called because they did not yet carry the record's official label art and information.
2. The term "wave" is commonly used to describe the different groupings of Detroit's techno artists, perhaps owing to its usage in Alvin Toffler's *The Third Wave.*
3. As Hawtin recalls, the club was "a really cheese, naff club" in Windsor called Hoppa's.
4. Hawtin's DJ name at the time was Richie Rich, after the comic book character.
5. There were several Detroit records that used Martin Luther King samples at this time, ranging from Reese & Santonio's brutal "Truth of Self-Evidence" to

May's unreleased "Martin," which was built around the bulk of King's "I Have a Dream" speech.

6. The Pro-One synthesizer was originally released by the Sequential Circuits company in 1980.

7. F.U.S.E. is an acronym for Futuristic Underground Subsonic Experiments, Hawtin's first solo project.

8. "Probe" was initially just "Pro," which was short for "Plus 8 Promotional Twelve-Inch."

9. Gianelli would eventually start his own label in association with Plus 8, called Telepathic.

10. John Williams, "1217," *Famzine.com,* January 25, 2006.

11. BFC is reportedly an acronym for Betty Ford Clinic. "Psyche" is pronounced like "psych," despite the mythological spelling.

12. Urban Tribe would resurface in 1996 on the influential London label Mo'Wax.

13. The terminology for industrial is just as complicated as that of techno. The term "industrial" was coined in 1976 by the group Throbbing Gristle, which used it to name its own record label, unaware that the term would come to define a fairly narrow slice of music.

14. According to attendees of a Front 242 concert in Detroit in 1990, Mills, who was also in the audience, was heavily influenced by the group's techno-industrial fusion and paramilitary stage gear.

15. The Wax Trax label brought several European industrial acts to the United States through a deal with Belgium's Play It Again Sam label.

16. The Final Cut took its name from the supposed "last" Pink Floyd album of the same name.

17. Some of these True Faith/Final Cut releases were on the Paragon sub-label Techno City.

18. Interfisch evolved into the label Tresor in 1991.

19. Named for their incorporation of mechanical sounds and synthesizers, the Mechanics also attempted to cover Kraftwerk songs live, playing their precise melodies and rhythms the hard way—by hand. One member, William Pope, was even dubbed "the Human Sequencer."

20. Joost DeLijser, "Jeff Mills," *Surreal Sound,* no. 5 (November 1993): 3.

21. Though "Waveform" has the catalog number UR004, it was actually only the label's third release (UR's catalog has a few numerical jumps and quirks). Mills had counted "The Theory," released on Retroactive in 1990, as the group's first release.

22. The labels on the WPA series read: "The World Power Alliance was formed on May 22, 1992, at 4:28 P.M."

23. The Red Planet's record labels credit only "the Martian" and, less frequently, guest artists like Eddie Fowlkes.

24. "Journey of the Dragons" features Juan Atkins on additional keyboards.

25. Langston would also end up recording hip-house for the Burdens' label as Metro D in 1991.

26. Hall is the great-great-grand-nephew of *Moby Dick* author Herman Melville, which is where the nickname "Moby" (which he's had since childhood) originated.

27. Murphy's mastering jobs can easily be spotted on vinyl via his tradesman-like "NSC" etching.

Chapter 6

1. Price left 808 State in 1992 to work as a producer.
2. Tommy Boy repackaged and reconfigured this album for the United States, releasing it as *808 Utd. State 90* in 1990.
3. LFO is an acronym for Low Frequency Oscillation.
4. "Interview with Fabrice Lig," *11th Hour Technology*, www.11-hour.com.
5. Jon Savage, "Machine Soul: A History of Techno," *Village Voice, Rock & Roll Quarterly Insert* (1993), http://music.hyperreal.org/library/machine_soul.html.
6. Subscription information located at http://music.hyperreal.org/lists/313/.
7. Coming full circle, Paxahau named Carl Craig creative director for Movement 2010.
8. Liz Warner, "WMC Interview: Carl Craig and the Future of Music," *Beatportal*, March 21, 2008, www.beatportal.com.

Chapter 7

1. The original term for this style—"jungle"—was at times taboo and smacked of a racial epithet.
2. *Urb* magazine gave Goldie this nickname in a 1996 cover story, highlighting him as a living link between hip-hop and its deconstructed, digital future.
3. On the album, "Timeless" is constructed of three parts: Inner City Life, Jah, and Pressure.
4. Jon Savage, *England's Dreaming: Anarchy, Sex Pistols, Punk Rock and Beyond* (New York: St. Martin's Press, 1992), 478.
5. Rob Young, "Getting Up to Speed," *The Wire*, no. 145 (March 1996).
6. Tortoise's McEntire wrote the score for the 1998 John Hughes film *Reach the Rock*.
7. A 1993 collaboration between Juan Atkins and German artist 3MB was even titled "Jazz Is the Teacher."
8. "Losing Control" was Bell's nod to the old Chicago classic "I've Lost Control" by Sleazy D.
9. It's unclear whether the term "minimal" was used prior to or only after Hood's release. Also, several Accelerate records were credited as "reduced by DBX," as opposed to "produced."
10. Jeff Mills, liner notes from *Axis: The Other Day*. This compilation of material recorded by Mills on his Axis label was released on React in 1997.
11. Wesley Crusher, "The Fly Guy," *Magic Feet*, no. 18 (July/August 1998): 13. (Please note that the name under which this article was written, "Wesley Crusher," is that of a character on the TV show *Star Trek: The Next Generation*, and is obviously an alias.)

12. Hari Kunzru, "Pirates Invade the Web," *Wired,* no. 5.12 (December 1997), www.com/wired/archive/5.12/es_pirate.html.

13. Hyperreal can be found at http://hyperreal.org.

14. FSOL also put out an edited version of their various "Net-casts" as the 1995 album *ISDN.*

Index

World Power Alliance (WPA), 103, 151
World 2 World, 104
Worrell, Bernie, 44
Wynn, Darrell "D," 54, 62, 93, 122

X-101, 104, 119
X-102, 104
XL Recordings, 117

Yamaha DX-100, 51
Yardbirds, 27

Yellow Magic Orchestra (YMO), 26, 76
Young, Claude, 61, 107
Young, Coleman, 35
Younghead, 136
Ypsilanti, 126, 127

Zapp, 26
Ze Records, 29
Zoth Ommog, 119